W9-AHH-602

THE GOSPEL OF MOSES

To
George and Helen —
In appreciation of
your interest in making this
Gospel available through the
printed page in this generation

Affectionately,

Sam

I John 4:19

9-20-74

THE GOSPEL OF

MOSES

SAMUEL J. SCHULTZ

HARPER & ROW, PUBLISHERS

New York   Evanston   San Francisco   London

To
Linda
Woody
David

FIRST EDITION

Library of Congress Cataloging in Publication Data

Schultz, Samuel J
  The gospel of Moses.
  Bibliography: p.
  1. Bible—History of Biblical events. 2. Moses.
I. Title.
BS635.2.S32 1974   225.9'5   74–4619
ISBN 0–06–067132–7
ISBN 0–06–067133–5 (pbk.)

CONTENTS

PREFACE

Is it possible to express the essence of the Bible in a few sentences or a short paragraph? From a dialogue between Jesus and the foremost learned leaders in Israel comes the most concise summary of the law and the prophets (the Old Testament) in two brief statements:

> Love God with all your heart
>
> Love your neighbor as yourself.

According to Jesus this epitomization not only expresses the essence of the written Bible available in His times but also stated the minimum requirement for any person who was concerned about life after death. Jesus answered the inquiring scribe, "Do this and you shall have eternal life."

The essence of this summary is recorded in the book of Deuteronomy. After years of study I came to the conclusion that Deuteronomy is the most important book in the Old Testament. Consequently after two decades of teaching I revised my methodology in sharing the Bible with my students by beginning Old Testament survey courses in Deuteronomy instead of Genesis. Consequently the following pages represent my personal interest in delineating this approach with those who may read these pages.

This summary provides an integrating core for understanding the Old Testament as a record of the God-man relationship that comes to a climax in Jesus Christ. Some read the Scriptures primarily as history or focus attention upon literary analysis. Frequently the Old Testament is viewed as law or undue emphasis is given to predictive prophecy. Recognition of the divine-human relationship offers a balance bringing various considerations of the Bible into a unifying perspective.

Is it reasonable to regard the Pentateuch, where this essence of God's requirements is recorded, as literature composed of legends, myths, fiction, and folklores? Is it possible in the light of modern scholarship to regard the account of Moses and his claim to have heard God speak to him as a reliable record?

In a previous volume *The Old Testament Speaks* I delineated the developments of God's revelation to Moses and subsequent prophets on the assumption that the Old Testament itself is a reliable and trustworthy account of events as they unfolded in the experiences of the Israelites. In these pages it is my concern to share in part with the reader a reasonable basis for this viewpoint in the light of current biblical scholarship.

It is the author's hope and prayer that each reader of this volume will turn anew to that which Moses and subsequent prophets recorded concerning God's relationship with man in Old Testament times. Quotations from the Bible represent various versions or the author's own translation.

S. J. SCHULTZ

Wheaton, Illinois
May 1974

1

THE MESSAGE OF
THE OLD TESTAMENT

Moses is the greatest man of Old Testament times. To him is attributed more than one-fourth of all the literature known today as the Old Testament. Exodus, Leviticus, Numbers, and Deuteronomy—directly associated with Moses himself—constitute a volume equal to the four Gospels plus the book of Acts. The Pentateuch is essential for the understanding of the rest of the Old Testament even as the four Gospels are basic to the rest of the New Testament.

The basic revelation of God's message to man came through Moses and was only surpassed and completed in the coming of Jesus Christ. Through Moses, God made known what was important for man to know about himself, his origin, his purpose in life Godward and manward, and his prospects for the future. What was revealed through the prophets following Moses was supplemental to and in agreement with the message of Moses.

The essence of the divine revelation at Mount Sinai is epitomized by Moses in the book of Deuteronomy. With a genuine concern for the Israelites' welfare as they anticipated crossing the Jordan into Canaan, Moses emphasized what was crucially significant for them as God's people. The book of Deuteronomy is often considered to be mere repetition because the word *deuteronomion*—which is based upon a mistaken understand-

1

ing of the words "copy of this law" (Deut. 17:18)—became the name of this book when it was translated into Greek in the third century B.C. Unfortunately this name has affected interpretation so that commentaries and introductory notes in study Bibles have emphasized that the book of Deuteronomy is a mere restatement of the law. Interestingly enough Jesus quoted this book more frequently and the New Testament writers refer to it more often than any other book in the Old Testament. When properly appraised in its historical context, the book of Deuteronomy emerges as the most important book in the entire Old Testament.

THE HISTORIC SETTING

Israel was encamped on the plains of Moab east of the Dead Sea and northward of the river Arnon. Almost four decades had passed since the Israelites left Egypt crossing the Red Sea into the Sinaitic desert. After a year's encampment at Mount Sinai they moved northward to Kadesh-barnea about forty miles south of Beersheba. From there twelve spies made an exploratory venture into Palestine, bringing back a pessimistic majority report concerning the prospects of conquest. Lacking faith in God and rebelling against Moses and Aaron as divinely appointed leaders, the Israelites were consigned to thirty-eight years of wandering in the wilderness. During this period all Israelites who had been over twenty years of age at the time of the Egyptian exodus were denied the prospects of entering Canaan and subject to death in the wilderness. The only exceptions were Joshua and Caleb.

The audience before Moses was a new generation consisting of Israelites under the age of sixty. Moses spoke to them on the basis of his experience with them through the last four decades as their leader. Together they had witnessed the greatest miracle of Israel's history in their deliverance from Egyptian bondage. Moses addressed them as one who had been the recipient of divine revelation at Mount Sinai as their representative. Consequently, what is recorded in the book of Deuteronomy is crucially significant not only for them but also for future generations throughout centuries and millenniums to follow.

The first four chapters of Deuteronomy are introductory and provide the background for the basic message. Moses in retrospect was not concerned about a survey of the past for the sake of history, but he opened this introduction by reviewing selected events beginning at Mount Horeb or Sinai. It was at Horeb that God revealed Himself to the Israelites. It was through Moses at Horeb that Israel was established in a divine relationship so that they might be God's chosen nation and a holy people in this world through whom God's salvation would be provided for all mankind. It was at Horeb that men of experience, wisdom, and discernment were appointed to aid in the administration of justice to govern their pattern of living as God's holy nation (1:13–18).

From Mount Horeb it was only an eleven days' journey to Kadesh-barnea, bringing them within reach of the land of promise. Through unbelief and rebellion, that generation forfeited their hopes and postponed Israel's prospects for nearly four decades. Moses repeatedly assured this new generation that they were to conquer and occupy the land God had promised to the patriarchs and their descendants (1:35ff.).

Moses emphasized the positive, pointing out how God had led and provided for them through the wilderness wanderings. Victory was already part of their experience through the conquest of the territory east of the river Jordan. This sample victory provided a basis for a reasonable faith that God would likewise enable them to conquer and occupy the land westward of the Jordan (3:21).

Wisdom for the Israelites consisted in doing what God expected them to do (4:6). In fact, Moses assured them they would be uniquely recognized as a wise nation if they lived in a relationship of obedience to God.

Unique among all nations was Israel in being recipients of God's revelation at Mount Horeb. This was unprecedented. This they should ever remember by continually responding in an attitude of reverence and respect for God. It was this attitude they should teach and impart to their children through precept and example (4:8–10). No other people had ever heard God speak to them as they had experienced and witnessed at Mount Horeb (4:32–40). Israel was the nation with whom the God of heaven and earth had identified Himself. The seriousness and sublimity of Israel's situation was unmatched. Moses was concerned that the Israelites realize this as he shared with them his parting message and instructions.

THE GOSPEL OF MOSES

Moses affirmed the divine revelation at Horeb in which God made a covenant with the Israelites. He was there as the mediator. He heard God speak and in turn he spoke to the people. Addressing the Israelites before him, he repeated the Ten Commandments which speak of exclusive devotion Godward and consideration for fellow men. In chapters 5 through 11, he elaborates almost exclusively on the former, expounding on Israel's covenantal kinship, its origin and prospects for continuity.

1. The First Commandment

Love is the key to a vital relationship with God. Love is the pivotal response of man to God in this God-man relationship established at Horeb. Listen to Moses in the opening words so well known as the Hebrew *Shema* in 6:5:

> And you shall love the Lord your God
>> with all your heart
>> with all your soul
>> with all your might.

Love involves a commitment. Love involves a way of life that expresses wholehearted exclusive devotion. Love, in its expression, taps all the resources of heart, soul, and all inner strength springing from man's entire being. It is this love and devotion to God that Moses emphasized as the way of life and success for the Israelites who had the prospects of entering Canaan before them.

Man's love for God is simply a response to God's love for him. God's love had first been exhibited generations earlier toward their ancestors (4:37; 7:7–8; 10:15; 33:3). God's love had been demonstrated in emancipating the Israelites from Egyptian bondage. On the basis of experiencing this love, Moses appealed to them to love God. Moses here anticipated what the New Testament writer expressed centuries later when God's love was manifested in Jesus, "We love him because he first loved us."

The realization that God loved them was to permeate their total pattern of living. Repeatedly they were to share with their children the fact that God had manifested His love in redeeming them from Egyptian bondage (4:10; 6:6–9; 11:13–21). In this manner they were to express their wholehearted devotion to God in daily life.

This love toward God must be exclusive. In the environmental culture of Egypt (from where they had come) and Canaan (where they were going), idols of every kind were worshiped and revered. Moses reminded them that

> I am the Lord your God who brought you
>   out of Egypt
>   out of the house of bondage
> You shall have no other gods before me (5:6–7).

God expected exclusive love and devotion in response to His love for them. This exclusive devotion was so important they were under obligation to stone anyone who posed as a prophet and advised the worship of other gods. Any consideration of or tolerance toward idolatry would affect and diminish their commitment to God and the love God expected in response to His love for them.

Man's relationship with God, Moses asserted, consisted of genuine love expressed in obedience. The older generation that died in the wilderness had failed to obey. They had rebelled against God (9:1–9:11). In spite of the disobedience and rebellion, Moses assured the people before him they would occupy the land of Canaan. They would not inherit the land because of their righteousness or merit it through their obedience, but simply on the basis that God was true to His promise made to the patriarchs (9:4–6). It was through God's goodness and love manifested toward them they would be enabled to occupy the land of Canaan. Never should they think they accomplished this through their own goodness or righteousness.

Obedience issues out of love. Moses did not emphasize a legalistic approach in meticulously conforming to minute details in ritual observances, sacrificial offerings, festive occasions and ceremonies. Religious activity motivated merely by obedience soon develops into legalism or a legalistic system. Religious activity motivated by love expresses a wholehearted devotion and commitment in a vital relationship with God. Consequently Moses was genuinely concerned that mutual love should prevail continually as the essence of this relationship between the Israelite and his God.

Consider Moses' summary appeal (10:12–22). Love Godward expressed in reverence, obedience, and service in daily life involving all resources of heart and soul constitutes the core of a right relationship with God. That this is not a legalistic or external matter was pinpointed by Moses in the admonition:

> Circumcise the foreskins of your heart
> Don't be stubborn any more (10:16).

It is not the external, covenantal sign of physical circumcision that is significant; it is the heart attitude that counts. Love toward God, an attitude of contrition and obedience, devotion to God untainted by idolatry, reverence and respect, permeated with a wholesome love for God—these, said Moses, were the essentials of life.

2. The Second Commandment

Brief, but significantly important, was the second concern of Moses expressed succinctly, "So show love for the alien" (10:19). God's people were to be known for their solicitous attitude toward those whose social and economic position exposed them to exploitation and oppression. The Mosaic law, permeated by a profound humanitarian spirit, stands in unique contrast to the Babylonian code of Hammurabi and the Assyrian and Hittite law codes of early times. These codes were not given through divine revelation.

Consider a brief comparison between the Code of Hammurabi and the laws given through Moses. In the former, property was so important that the penalty for theft was death, while the latter required restitution (Exod. 22:1,4). The Babylonians were concerned with protecting the interests of the rich, charging high interest rates, while in Israel usury was prohibited (Exod. 22:25–27). While the former provided for the return of slaves to the owners, the Mosaic regulation respected slavery and implied compassionate treatment for slaves (Exod. 21:1–10; Deut. 23:15–16). Slaves could voluntarily become part of an Israelite family (Exod. 21:5–60). An Israelite was duty-bound to return a straying animal even to an enemy (Exod. 23:4).

In Israel, crimes against fellow men were considered to be crimes against God, who could give and take life. Consequently life was more important than property. If an ox gored a man in the open street, Babylonian law required no payment. If an ox killed a member of the aristocracy or a slave, the fine was one-half or one-third mina respectively. Israelite law by contrast demanded that a goring ox be stoned to death and the owner as well if he was found to be negligent. Since the death penalty was carried out by stoning by the community, no individual was responsible for killing as the Israelites conformed to the commands of God who was responsible for giving and taking life.

Originating with a compassionate God (Exod. 22:27) the Israelite laws were generally kind and humane. If a creditor took the outer cloak of a poor man for a loan, the garment had to be returned before sunset (Exod. 22:26–27).

This second commandment issues out of man's relationship toward God. It is God who executes justice for orphans and widows and provides food and clothing for them (10:17–18). The Israelites had experienced oppression and slavery in Egypt. Having been the recipients of God's redeeming love, they are now admonished to express this love that they have experienced toward those about them. They are to reflect the justice of God in their relationship with others.

In the context of this commandment, "Love your neighbor as yourself" in Leviticus (19:10–19), the emphasis is upon a holy and just God. Man's vertical relationship with God is to be evident in a horizontal relationship with his fellow men. A holy God expects justice and righteousness to prevail toward strangers and aliens.

In Deuteronomy 12–26, Moses interprets and applies these two basic laws to the pattern of everyday living. In anticipation of immediate entrance into Canaan, he adapted his instructions to the practical aspects of occupation and settlement in the land of promise. Numerous laws and regulations were modified in view of this transition from a migratory situation to a permanent state. Love for God and love for man should be reflected in all their relationships.

Appropriately Moses led his people in a service of confession (chap. 26). Through acts of dedication and reaffirmation of the covenant, the people renewed their commitment to God as a nation, making them all conscious again of their unique relationship to God and their particular responsibility to live as God's holy people. The previous generation had ratified their covenant with God at Mount Horeb (Exod. 24:7). Having outlined the principles essential for living as God's chosen nation, Moses here publicly involved this new generation in the renewal of the covenant. He assured them they would be the foremost of all nations if they would continually maintain an attitude of love and wholehearted commitment toward God.

Keenly aware of the fact that a covenantal promise must be continually renewed and maintained in daily life, Moses instructed the Israelites to renew this covenant under Joshua publicly once they entered Canaan (27:1–26). Impressively, he delineated the two alternatives—the way of blessing and the way of cursing—before his audience (28:1–68). With a personal appeal unique in history, Moses solemnly implored them— men, women, children, non-Israelites and servants—to recognize what God had done for them and to respond by choosing the right way so they would continue to be recipients of God's blessings (29:1–29). Idolatry—an outward sign of a lack of exclusive devotion toward God—would result in failure and exile. If exile should be their lot because of disobedience, Moses pointed to repentance as the way back to God. Moses assured them that if they repented God would "circumcise your heart and the heart of your descendants, to love the Lord your God with all your heart and with all your soul in order that you may live." Out of this relationship with "the Lord your God"—a title occurring no fewer than twelve times in 30:1–10—obedience will normally follow.

The Israelites had to make the decision—a crucial one. They had the freedom of choice. If they chose to love God, they would enjoy the blessings divinely promised to them. If they decided not to love God, the curse awaited them. Ultimately it was a matter of choosing the way of life or choosing the way of death (30:11–20).

The final chapters of Deuteronomy (31–34) provide for the

transfer of leadership to Joshua as the divinely appointed successor to Moses. In written form Moses provided a copy of "this law," entrusting it to the priests responsible for the ark of the covenant. From this written copy, that which had been revealed to Moses was to be communicated periodically to the coming generations so they might learn to reverence God in love and obedience. With a parting song and testament for his people, Moses—"the servant of the Lord" who knew the Lord "face to face"—died.

PROPHETS THAT FOLLOW

The message revealed to and summarized by Moses provided the basis for all the true prophets in Israel throughout Old Testament times. Whatever divine revelation came to succeeding prophets was in agreement with and supplementary to that which had been revealed through Moses.

Samuel was called to be a prophet in times when the religion of Israel had declined to a naturalistic perspective and the Israelites were oppressed by the Philistines. With the people assembled before him, Samuel confronted them with the simple basic proposition, "If you return to the Lord . . ." (I Sam. 7:3). Moses' first commandment has been disregarded.

Isaiah opened his message by bringing the first commandment of Moses into focus. Surrounded by a society permeated by social injustice as well as idolatry, he identified the basic problem, charging that the Israelites have

> revolted against me (1:2)
> abandoned the Lord
> despised the Holy One of Israel
> turned away from him (1:4).

Adjustment to God is the starting point for adjusting relationships with one another.

Another example is Jeremiah. His fundamental concern

when impending doom awaited Jerusalem was that the people have forsaken God (2:13). This was the basic evil. Consequently Jeremiah addressed himself largely to warning the people that they had broken their relationship with God. The outward form of religion was of no avail as long as they did not renew their devotion exclusively to God. Cultic apostasy was at the heart of Israel's condition, subject to divine judgment.

The breaking of the second commandment of Moses—*love your neighbor*—is very pronounced throughout the preaching of the prophets. Consider how Isaiah (1–5), Amos (1–9), Hosea, Jeremiah, and many others attack the injustice and the social evils so evident in the times in which they lived. Oppression of the poor, neglect of the widows and orphans, cheating, stealing, inequitable business practices—these and many other problems in daily life were constantly under examination as the prophets reminded the people they should "prepare to meet God," as pointedly expressed by Amos. Mistreatment of their fellow men was a violation of the Mosaic command to permeate daily relationships with the love that issued from a vital relationship Godward.

JESUS AND THE GOSPEL OF MOSES

Jesus in His teaching specifically identified the gospel of Moses as the basis for eternal life. When a lawyer of the Pharisees posed man's basic question, "What must I do to inherit eternal life?" Jesus pointed to the two fundamental laws—*love God with all your heart and your neighbor as yourself* (Luke 10:25–28).

In the context of discussing these as the two greatest commandments (Matt. 22:34–40), Jesus made a very significant observation as to how they relate to the Old Testament. He asserted that these two laws are the essence or core of the law and the prophets—an identification of the entire literature known now as the Old Testament. The heart of the entire written revelation can be summarized in these two great commandments.

According to the account given by Mark (12:28–34), the scribe voluntarily suggested that these two laws were so basic that the offering of sacrifices was of secondary significance. In view of the legalism of contemporary Judaism at the time of Jesus—some 613 laws as oral tradition and later transmitted in written form—this agreement between Jesus and the scribe is very important and significant. Jesus not only concurs, commending the scribe for his intelligent answer, but also assures him he is "not far from the kingdom" when he recognizes from his intellectual perspective that the two great commandments do not consist of a legalistic fulfillment of the law but are vital as a love relationship toward God and man.

Jesus not only taught these two great commandments as the essence of what was important, but He also came to fulfill the law by observing them. Jesus exemplified a wholehearted devotion to and love for God in His daily life and gave His life voluntarily for others. No greater love was ever exhibited in anyone before Him. In this way Jesus was more than a prophet and thus exceeded Moses, through whom the greatest revelation from God had come in Old Testament times. Jesus constituted the fullness of God's revelation.

II

THE HISTORIC
REVELATION

Unique and without precedent was the historic event in which God revealed Himself to the Israelites at Mount Horeb or Sinai. Keenly aware of the uniqueness of this event, Moses focused attention upon the historic occasion in his farewell addresses to the Israelites on the Moab plains.

Two things he wanted them to remember in particular (Deut. 4:10, 33–36). They had actually heard God speak as they stood before Mount Sinai—an experience no other people had witnessed. They had been miraculously taken out of another nation —no other nation had ever experienced anything like it. Israel's God had emancipated them from Egyptian bondage and had audibly spoken to them encamped in the desert. The former was the outstanding miracle never surpassed in Old Testament times. The divine revelation at Sinai was exceeded only by the coming of Jesus Christ as the manifestation of God's love.

THE EMANCIPATION

Crucial to the emancipation of Israel was the leadership of Moses. He was the key figure in the developments that brought about the deliverance of the Israelites from the enslavement by the Egyptians.

Born in troublesome times, Moses was providentially exposed to the religious training of an Israelite home and the educational and cultural opportunities available to him in the court of the king of Egypt. Frustrated in his attempts to help his people, he fled to the Midian desert where he made his living as a herdsman for a Midian priest named Jethro whose daughter, Zipporah, Moses married (Exod. 1–2).

Moses received a divine call to leadership (Exod. 3–4). It was God who broke the silence and spoke to Moses out of a burning bush that appeared to him to be an eternal flame. God initiated the conversation and identified Himself in history which was meaningful to Moses:

> I am the God of your father
> the God of Abraham
> the God of Isaac
> the God of Jacob.

The assignment God had for Moses was explicit and direct, "I will send you to Pharaoh, so that you may bring My people, the sons of Israel out of Egypt."

From personal experience and observation, Moses knew better than anyone else what was involved in contesting the power of the mighty king of Egypt who was second to none in the Fertile Crescent at that time. Looking at his own resources and abilities, he felt very inadequate to accept this responsibility. He knew from his own experience he would have difficulty in gaining a favorable hearing or the support of the Israelites and he was certain that Pharaoh would not take orders from him.

God did not leave Moses to his own resources. He was commissioned by the I AM WHO I AM (also translated "I was" or "I will be" or "I bring to pass"). The eternal, ever-present God who had spoken to Abraham, Isaac, and Jacob was sending Moses to fulfill the promise that Israel was to be delivered from Egypt and brought into the land of Canaan. To verify Moses' claim that the God of the patriarchs had sent him, Moses was endowed with the ability to perform two signs: the staff-serpent-staff miracle and the leprous-hand miracle. When Moses returned to Egypt he performed these miracles before the Israelites to assure them that God was about to deliver them from Egypt. Their response was:

> So the people believed: and when they heard that the Lord was concerned about the sons of Israel and that He had seen their affliction, then they bowed low and worshiped (Exod. 4:31).

The confrontation with Pharaoh looked like a hopeless task from the human perspective. During the New Kingdom era (*ca.* 1570–1085 B.C.) the Egyptians extended their political and economic control through Palestine up to the Euphrates, maintaining a powerful kingdom along the Nile that was second to none in the Ancient Near East. God had informed Moses (Exod. 3) that the king of Egypt would not permit the Israelites to leave "except under compulsion." Moses also received the assurance that God would strike Egypt with miracles compelling Pharaoh to release the Israelites.

The plagues brought the judgment of God upon the Egyptians as Moses faced Pharaoh with the request to release the Israelites. The first nine plagues are distinctly associated with the natural phenomena in the Nile Valley beginning with an unusually high flood in July or August. The effects of such an excessive inundation would have lasted into October or November, leaving an abundance of dead fish to plague the Egyptians. Swarms of frogs dying en masse, lice or gnats in abundance, swarms of insects or flies plaguing the people, severe pestilence on livestock, fine dust causing boils to erupt in open sores on man as well as beast, a heavy hail destroying barley and flax in February, swarms of locusts in March to consume new growth, and an extraordinary dust storm, making the air so thick and dark that it obscured the light of the sun for three days—these were the plagues that came in sequence and confronted Pharaoh with the God of the Israelites. The miraculous element in this process was evident in the intensity, timing, and duration. The power of Israel's God was portrayed and demonstrated during this period in contrast to the impotence of the many gods of Egypt.

In the course of these plagues, Pharaoh resisted and hardened his heart. Given the opportunity to comply with the request to let the Israelites go, he became more determined and obstinate every time he refused. From the larger perspective "the Lord hardened Pharaoh's heart." God entrusted him with life and the opportunity to rule Egypt. Had God caused him to die before Moses and Aaron came to his court, Pharaoh would not have been exposed to the events during which he resisted, nor would he have had the opportunity to comply with the will of God. His attitude, however, was defiant at the very beginning when he replied to Moses' request, "Who is the Lord that I should obey His voice to let Israel go? I do not know the Lord, and besides I will not let Israel go" (Exod. 5:2).

The tenth and final plague was wholly supernatural. Through the death of the firstborn, divine judgment was executed "against all the gods of Egypt." Although the control of God over natural creation had been in evidence as Moses announced the successive plagues occurring with growing severity, Pharaoh intensified his resistance and refused to acknowledge God. The clearest credentials of God's authority and power were apparent in the precise and full control in the death of only the first-born in each family in Egypt. Having been duly warned about this impending plague, Pharaoh together with his people was subjected to the consequences of refusal.

For the Israelites this tenth plague marked the hour of their deliverance from slavery. Being informed by Moses of this impending divine judgment, the Israelites were instructed to kill a lamb for each household and prepare a meal to be eaten in preparation for the exodus. The blood of the lamb applied to the doorposts of each home where a family was assembled for this occasion provided the visible sign to exclude them from the death of the first-born at midnight. This ceremony was called the Lord's Passover and was to be observed annually ever after this in memory of the fact that the Lord had passed over them when this plague brought death to each household of the Egyptians.

When the plague struck at midnight, Pharaoh urged Moses and the Israelites to leave. Aided by the Egyptians, the Israelites migrated toward the Red Sea, or Sea of Reeds, and not along the Mediterranean coast, which was the natural and shortest route to the land of Canaan. When they reached the sea the Israelites witnessed the mighty acts of God in their behalf. Pharaoh had changed his mind once more and pursued the Israelites but was prevented from overtaking them by the manifestation of God's presence appearing as a pillar of cloud by day and a pillar of fire by night. Before them the Israelites witnessed the miraculous power of God in evidence as a strong east wind opened a way for them through the sea. Subsequently the Israelites saw the Egyptian army submerged as they attempted to follow them.

In this manner the mighty acts of God were displayed in the emancipation of the Israelites. The power of God had been operative through the created order as well as through direct miraculous intervention. Through this experience of deliverance "the people revered the Lord and came to believe in the Lord and in His servant Moses" (Exod. 14:31).

With the Red Sea and the Egyptians behind them, the Israelites moved southward, divinely led by a luminous cloud. The material provisions of water, manna, and quails provided a daily reminder of God's care for them en route to Mount Sinai.

GOD SPEAKS TO ISRAEL

Mount Sinai has historic significance for Israel. It was here that the greatest revelation of God occurred in Old Testament times. It was here that Israel was established as an independent nation. It was here that the covenant between God and Israel was ratified. It was here that the covenant was committed to writing, giving birth to the canon of the Old Testament.

Redemption from the bondage of Egypt preceded the covenant. The divine promises made to the patriarchs that their descendants would return to Canaan had been partially fulfilled. They were on their way to the promised land. The display of God's power in their deliverance from the power of Pharaoh provided a rational basis for their faith in God and Moses as His representative.

God had chosen the patriarchs and their descendants to be His chosen nation. God had redeemed the Israelites out of Egyptian bondage to be "my own possession among all the peoples . . . to be a kingdom of priests and a holy nation" (Exod. 19:5–6). Now God wanted to speak to Moses and the people "in order that the people may hear when I speak with you, and may also believe in you forever" (Exod. 19:9). By speaking audibly so all the people could hear, God confirmed Moses as the mediator and gave him special credentials before the whole nation. What God spoke here was the fundamental law of the covenant and possessed everlasting validity (Matt. 5:18).

Awesome indeed was the promulgation of the words of God. Audibly they were spoken by Him so all Israel could hear (Exod. 20:1–17). Duplicate copies—each copy contained the complete Decalogue—on tablets of stone "written by the finger of God" (Exod. 31:18) were given to Moses who subsequently shattered them on his way down from the mount of revelation. Later Moses made written copies of these words which were deposited in the ark of the covenant (Exod. 34:27–28; 40:20; Deut. 10:5).

"Covenant" or "words of the agreement" (Exod. 34:28; Deut. 4:13) is the most appropriate designation of "these words" audibly spoken by God in the presence of Israel. Moses identifies this covenant (Deut. 4:13) with the "tablets of the covenant" (Deut. 9:9, 11, 15).

"Testimony" is equally appropriate to designate God's

spoken words (Exod. 25:16, 21; 40:20). The written copies were deposited by the ark which was repeatedly identified as "ark of the testimony" in Exodus and "ark of the covenant" in Numbers and Deuteronomy. The ark was located in the most holy place in the tabernacle.

Although "Ten Commandments" or "Decalogue" is used several times (Exod. 34:10; Deut. 4:13; 10:4) it is unfortunate that this has become the most common and often exclusive designation for this audible revelation by God to Israel. This designation has been the basis for a legalistic interpretation of God's spoken words and has often obscured the real nature of what He communicated in this message.

From the literary analysis the "words of God" (Exod. 20:1–17) are expressed in the literary pattern of Hittite treaties made between suzerain and vassal and not in the legalistic framework of the codes of law such as those of Hammurabi, Lipit Ishtar, and others common to the ancient Near East. Current knowledge of these vassal treaties provides enlightenment for a better understanding of "these words" that God spoke to Israel as given in the context of Exodus 19–24.

Six similarities emerge as common to the suzerainty treaties and God's covenant with Israel. In the preamble would appear the name, titles, and attributes of the great king to establish his identity. God identifies Himself as, "I am the Lord your God." The historical prologue provided the background or historical developments for the treaty. God appropriately spoke as "the Lord your God who brought you out of the land of Egypt, out of the house of slavery." Next followed the stipulations or obligations of the vassal to the king. These are expressed basically in Exodus 20:2–17 and expanded in 20:18–23:33. Ratification of the treaty was vitally important. Israel's response (Exod. 24) was to accept this covenant formally, followed by sacrifices and offerings and finally the covenant meal. In Hittite treaties usually a list of gods was included as witnesses to such an agreement. Israel did not recognize gods but in Deuteronomy (4:26; 30:19;

31:28; 32:1) "heaven and earth" are considered as witnesses to the covenant. Deposition and public proclamation were also very important. A suzerain usually provided two copies of the treaty—one to be deposited in the temple of his god and one to be placed in the temple of the vassal's god. Israel's duplicate copies were stored by the ark in the tabernacle and read publicly every seven years as indicated in Deuteronomy. Curse and blessing were included in the treaty and awaited the vassal, depending on his actions in maintaining the agreement. Israel was warned of God's curse (Exod. 20:5) and assured of His blessing (20:6). These were expanded in the immediate context and more elaborately in Deuteronomy.

Relationship—not law—is the key to understanding the two tablets of stone conveying God's words to man. God's covenantal relationship with the nation He had delivered out of Egypt was established and confirmed here in this divine utterance. This covenant rested on the promise previously made to the patriarchs and now was publicly confirmed to Israel as a newly established nation (Exod. 2:24; 4:22; 6:6–8). This relationship is basic to a proper interpretation of all the laws, stipulations, and instructions given to Israel.

This relationship preceded the law, or Ten Commandments. The law did not establish this covenant but was intended to govern or regulate this relationship which existed by faith. For the Israelites who heard God speak, there was evidence of their redemption from Egypt and the sound of God's voice to provide a rational basis for their faith. The law pointed the way of life and not a way to gain life. The law was neither the focal point nor the core of Israel's relationship with God, but was part of the covenant.

The Ten Commandments are basic stipulations concisely expressing God's will for His people in maintaining this relationship. They are closely connected with the historical prologue. The first four commandments express the responsibility the individual Israelite has to his God. Love and loyalty to God are absolutely essential if this relationship is to continue between him and God. The six commandments that follow regulate man's behavior toward other members of society. Love and respect for others issue out of God's concern for them. God's love and holiness are to be reflected in the life of the God-revering person in his relationship with his fellow men. Out of man's vertical relationship with God issues proper horizontal relationship toward his neighbor.

This spiritual relationship with God occupied the central place in the audible communication from God to man in the Sinai revelation. The words of this covenant that cemented this relationship were not legalistic but brought the imperatives of the reality of God's holiness to bear upon the people in regulating their communion and continued enjoyment of God's blessing. Holy living issued out of this covenantal relationship. Redemption or salvation came first through the manifestation of God's love in their emancipation. Next came the establishment of the covenant in which love, loyalty, and exclusive devotion mutually prevailed between God and man. In the context of this relationship, obedience to the divinely given instructions and laws became a way of life.

Israel's religion was a revealed religion. Beyond this basic revelation in which love for God and love for man were delineated as the essence of a vital relationship Godward, there came through Moses instructions that would enable the Israelites to live as God's holy people. A tabernacle was to be created with its various parts and furniture providing a place of worship and a depository for the written copies of the covenant. The priesthood was organized with Aaron as the high priest and the Levites as his assistants. Various offerings were prescribed for the nation in daily sacrifice and for the individual as needed or desired. Appointed feasts and seasons were scheduled throughout the year which repeatedly by the nature of their observance brought a consciousness of God into the pattern of everyday living.

The tabernacle, the priesthood, the offerings and the numerous religious observances were merely the means to an end. When the Israelites focused attention upon the external rituals and observances, then religion drifted into formality and often hypocrisy. Morals were lowered to a human perspective as God was obscured from daily life. In the course of time, prophet after prophet recognized this in the times in which he lived and charged the Israelites with breaking their covenant relationship with God. The crux of the problem usually was found in the words God asked Moses to convey to the Israelites in the context of the Sinai revelation, ". . . if you will indeed obey My voice and keep My covenant, then you shall be My own possession among all the peoples, for all the earth is Mine; and you shall be to Me a kingdom of priests and a holy nation" (Exod. 20:5–6). The keeping of the covenant—maintaining a vital relationship with God—was the cord of life for the Israelite.

III

THE FATHERS
OF ISRAEL

At the burning bush God identified Himself to Moses as "the God of Abraham, the God of Isaac, and the God of Jacob" (Exod. 3:6). Four decades later on the Moab plains, Moses appropriately reminded the new generation anticipating entrance into Canaan that God had spoken to the whole nation of Israel at Mount Sinai

> because
>> He loved your fathers,
> therefore
>> He chose their descendants after them
> And
>> He personally brought you from Egypt . . . (Deut. 4:37).

Moses asserts that they are a holy people divinely chosen to enter Canaan "because the Lord loved you and kept the oath which He swore to your forefathers" (Deut. 7:8–13).

How did God show His love to their patriarchal fathers? How did God reveal Himself to Abraham, Isaac, and Jacob? What did God promise to Abraham and his descendants? The record of this divine-human relationship is recorded in the book of Genesis (chaps. 12–50). Unique indeed was this divine revelation as it unfolded in the lives of Abraham, Isaac, Jacob, and Joseph.

Fascinating and intriguing are the life situations in which these men struggled and often conformed to their contemporary culture and yet responded to divine revelation and guidance. Encouraging for the reader is the fact that, even with their failures and human weaknesses, they responded to God's love and promises in faith and obedience that made them conscious of a vital relationship with God and a hope for the future. They reflect the tensions of God-fearing people living in a godless culture.

ABRAHAM—FRIEND OF GOD

Abraham's ancestors worshiped idols (Josh. 24:2). Idolatry at Ur, where they may have resided before migrating to Haran, dominated the culture of the Third Dynasty of Ur whose king Ur-Nammu built a ziggurat—a tower 70 feet high with a solid mass of brickwork base 200 by 150 feet—for the shrine of Nannar the moon-god. Among the temples in the sacred area surrounding the ziggurat was the Gig-par-ku temple dedicated to Ningal the wife of Nannar.

Business facilities, factories, workshops, provisions for food, offerings, the court of law, and other common interests constituted this commercial as well as religious center for the populace at large. Beyond this the city of Ur, which covered about 150 acres, had a residential area with an estimated population of about twenty-four thousand.

At Haran, located some six hundred miles north on the Balikh branch of the Euphrates River, the culture was similar to that of Ur, very likely also devoted to the worship of the moon-god Nannar. Haran was a flourishing city in Abraham's time and even twentieth-century Muslims in that area assert that their lineage goes back to Abraham. En route from Ur to Haran, Abraham's family may have passed through the Euphrates river city of Mari, an outstanding center of culture in Mesopotamia flourishing several centuries before it was conquered by Hammurabi about 1700 B.C. In this city idolatry was reflected in a ziggurat with a temple dedicated to Ishtar.

Abraham emerged from the idolatrous culture of his times by leaving Haran and migrating some five hundred miles west and south into the land of Canaan. This migration can only be explained as Abraham's response to a divine call (Gen. 12:1–3) and as a purposeful obedience expressing his faith in God. How this initial message was communicated to Abraham is not stated in the biblical account, but that Abraham responded to God's promise is repeatedly asserted in subsequent generations.

Distinctive and unique in the culture of his times is Abraham's devotion to God. Repeatedly it is recorded that he erected an altar, giving witness to the idolatrous community in which he lived that he was worshiping the God of heaven and earth. Throughout his life he seems to have communication with God in such a realistic manner that he is later identified as a "friend" of God (Isa. 41:8; Jas. 3:23).

After leaving his homeland in Mesopotamia, Abraham lived in Canaan for about a century. Considering the length of his life and the brevity of the account in Genesis (chaps. 12–25) the reader is impressed with the extensive consideration given to the divine revelations contained in the conversations between God and Abraham. The initial promises made to Abraham to which he responded in obedience were enlarged and confirmed, and often specific instructions were given to guide him in facing the tensions he encountered in the cultural situation of everyday life.

Consider the prospect for the future given initially to Abraham when God said

> I will
> make you a great nation
> bless you
> make your name great so you shall be a blessing
> bless those who bless you

    curse those who curse you
  And in you shall all the families of the earth be blessed
    (Gen. 12:1–3).

It was on the basis of these promises that Abraham left his culture, his family, and the fertile valley of the Euphrates to live as a stranger in the land of Canaan. Arriving at Shechem, Abraham erected an altar expressing his love and wholehearted devotion to God.

Although a famine caused Abraham to migrate down to Egypt for a brief period, he together with his nephew Lot prospered exceedingly in the land of Canaan. When tension developed because of the increase of their livestock, Lot was given the choice and decided to move eastward to the fertile plains of Sodom. After this traumatic experience of separating from Lot, divine confirmation and reassurance came to Abraham (Gen. 13:14–17). His descendants would be as numerous as the dust of the earth and inherit the land in which he was living. Once again Abraham built an altar to the Lord.

When Abraham was seriously considering appointing Eliezer, his servant from Damascus, as his heir in accordance with the legal provisions in contemporary culture, God promised him a son. Through this son the descendants of Abraham would become as numerous as the stars of heaven. On a starlit night one can count about four thousand stars with the naked eye in the heavens above Canaan. Whether or not Abraham considered counting the stars is not indicated, but the record simply states that he "believed in the Lord." This expression of confidence and faith in God was credited to Abraham as righteousness (15:1–6).

God made a covenant with Abraham (15:7–21). In contemporary culture sometimes a suzerain would commit himself to an oath, especially so in case of a land grant. God here identifies Himself—as was customary in standard treaty patterns—as "the Lord who brought you out of Ur of the Chaldees." The ritual for ratifying the oath reflected contemporary customs. In the expansion of God's covenant came the forewarning of Egyptian enslavement and the divine judgment upon the Egyptians and the Amorites.

Twenty-four years had passed since Abraham settled in Canaan. Humanly speaking Abraham and Sarah had no realistic hopes for having descendants, as long as they had no son. Lot and Eliezer had been eliminated as heirs. Ishmael, who had been born to Abraham and an Egyptian maid, Hagar, was a teenager with the prospects of being the heir according to the cultural customs prevailing in the Near East. It is in this situation that God enlarges the covenant with Abraham for his ratification.

In this divine revelation (Gen. 17:1–18:15) the promises of God are expanded, special guidance is given to him concerning the problems relating to Ishmael, the promise of a son to Abraham and Sarah is renewed, and Abraham receives specific instructions to ratify the covenant by oath.

The promise of the land to Abraham's descendants is renewed with the assurance that God Almighty will be their God. With this promise in view, God's practical advice to Abraham was to "live ever mindful of My presence" or "walk in My ways and be blameless." God's blessing is promised to all of Abraham's descendants including Ishmael. The lineage through Sarah's son, however, has the covenantal promise of royalty. Circumcision which was practiced earlier in contemporary society was now made the sign of incorporation into the Abrahamic covenant. By administering circumcision to himself and all his household, Abraham confirmed the oath and thereby acknowledged the Lordship of God. During the meal with the three heavenly visitors, which may have been the confirmation of the covenant, the promise of a son to Abraham and Sarah was assured fulfillment and that within one year's time.

Sublime and unique was the divine revelation concerning Sodom and Gomorrah (18:16–19:29). God confides in Abraham

—whose descendants were to exemplify justice and righteousness and bring divine blessings to all nations—the fact that these cities are doomed pending further examination. It is in the awesomeness of this moment that Abraham emerges as an intercessor. He prays, however, in the confidence that "the Judge of all the earth will deal justly."

Isaac, the promised son, was born to Abraham and Sarah (Gen. 21). Now that Sarah had her own son, she coveted sole heirship for Isaac even though, according to the laws, Ishmael was entitled to share in the inheritance. Legally it was also possible to have Ishmael's inheritance rights waived for his mother Hagar's freedom but she could not be sold as a slave since she had borne a son for her master. Consequently Sarah insisted that Abraham coerce Hagar and Ishmael to choose freedom. Reluctantly considering Sarah's advice, Abraham complied, being divinely assured that Ishmael would become a great nation but that the covenant would be confirmed through Isaac.

The climactic, crucial test in the divine-human relationship came when Abraham was instructed by God to offer his only son Isaac (22:1–19). Abraham faced the conflict between obedience (which in this case would seemingly eliminate the prospects for descendants and the fulfillment of the covenantal promise) and hope (the possibility that God would restore the life to Isaac after he was sacrificed) by faith in God. Ascending the mount of sacrifice together, Isaac asked his father the piercing, probing question, "Here are the fire and the wood, but where is the lamb for the burnt offering?" Abraham reached beyond the point of reason or rationalization and gave an answer that expressed his utmost confidence and faith in God by replying, "God will provide for Himself the lamb for the burnt offering, my son." Through this obedience, Abraham demonstrated the truth of his oath of unreserved allegiance to God. Abraham was wholly devoted to God and demonstrated his love and devotion through obedience. Once again the covenantal promise was audibly confirmed to Abraham with the divine commendation, ". . . because you have obeyed Me."

So important was this divine promise that he exacted an oath from his servant that he would not take Isaac out of Canaan under any circumstances. Since Abraham did not want Isaac to marry a Canaanite woman, the servant was instructed to secure a bride from Mesopotamia. In response to the questions and problems his servant raises, Abraham reflected his confidence and faith in God by replying, "The Lord, the God of heaven, who took me from my father's house and the land of my birth . . . He will send His angel before you, and you will take a wife for my son from there."

ISAAC—THE PROMISED HEIR

To Isaac the promise made to Abraham was confirmed by divine revelation (Gen. 26). When the pressure of famine caused Isaac to move to Gerar, the Lord warned him not to go down to Egypt but to remain in the land of Canaan. At this time the Lord assured him that

> I will be with you
>> bless you
>> give these lands to your descendants
>> establish the oath I swore to Abraham
>> make your seed as many as the stars in the sky
>> bless all nations through your descendants (26:3–4).

All of this God promised Isaac "because of My promise to Abraham who obeyed Me."

Pressed by the economic and cultural circumstances at Gerar, Isaac moved to Beersheba. There God identified Himself as "I am the God of your father Abraham" and reaffirmed His presence and blessing upon Isaac and his family "for the sake of my servant Abraham." Isaac responded to this renewal of covenantal guarantees by building an altar and worshiping

God. Through this experience the Philistines recognized that
God was with Isaac. Subsequently a covenant they had previously had with Abraham was renewed with Isaac.

Isaac reflected the stewardship of covenantal promises as he
gave his blessing to Jacob (Gen. 27). The Abraham-Isaac succession was bestowed upon Jacob confirming the prenatal predictions that the older should serve the younger. Included in this
blessing were the basic promises of the land of Canaan and the
pivotal role the descendants of Jacob would have in the blessings and curses upon all other nations.

When the exigencies of life caused Jacob to leave Canaan and
flee to Mesopotamia the patriarchal heritage was impressed
upon him by Isaac in the prayer ". . . May God Almighty bless
you. . . . May He also give you the blessing of Abraham. . . ." En
route at Bethel, Jacob experienced personal confirmation in a
divine revelation in which God spoke, "I am the Lord, the God
of your father Abraham and the God of Isaac." With this identification came the reassurance that he and his descendants
would possess Canaan and that God's presence would be with
him to fulfill these divine promises.

JACOB—FATHER OF ISRAEL

During the years that Jacob lived in Mesopotamia or Paddan-
Aram, the land of his mother's birth, he prospered greatly so
that he was enriched with a large family and material wealth
consisting of flocks and herds (Gen. 29–30). Sensitive to the
unfriendly attitude of his father-in-law, Laban, Jacob made
plans to move back to Canaan (Gen. 31). He recognized that
"the God of my father has been with me" and as divine revelation the consciousness that "the God of Bethel" was instructing
him "to return to the land of his birth." En route he faced
several significant crises.

Laban, who overtook Jacob in Gilead—some three hundred
miles from Paddan-Aram—accused Jacob of stealing the

household idols, possession of which provided some legal advantage as to inheritance. Being divinely restrained, Laban did not deal as harshly with Jacob as he had planned previously in pressing his enforceable legal claims against him. Frustrated in his search, Laban arranged a mutual nonaggression pact which would prevent Jacob from making an inheritance claim in case he did have the idols in his possession. A pillar or cairn was erected with God as witness—"May the Lord watch between you and me"—that neither of them would pass this point after this agreement. After a meal sealing this pact, Laban returned to Mesopotamia.

Approaching Canaan, Jacob faced the threat of his revengeful brother Esau (Gen. 32–33). In view of the ominous report that Esau was coming to meet him with four hundred men, Jacob resorted to defensive tactics commonly adopted by caravans, dividing all his possession into two units hoping one would be spared in case of attack. As "your servant Jacob" he sent gifts to appease Esau, hoping for kind treatment. Then Jacob prayed, ". . . deliver me, I pray, from my brother Esau, for I am afraid he may come and destroy me including my family . . ." (32:-9–12). He sent all of his possessions and family across the river Jabbok while he remained behind.

Jacob was alone that night—perhaps to ponder the seriousness of the situation. He could not return to Mesopotamia, and the threat of revenge by a force too powerful for him threatened his return to his homeland. So far in life Jacob had seemingly solved all problems to his advantage. In the solitude of this night on the brink of Jabbok he wrestled with a man and seemingly overcame him. However, this man left Jacob with a wrenched hip. In the encounter when Jacob exacted a blessing he was informed that since he had prevailed as a prince with God and man, his name was changed to Israel reflecting this experience of contending with God (cf. Hos. 12:4). Realizing he had encountered God that night, he named the place Peniel, meaning "face of God." Although Jacob was victor in the struggle and obtained a blessing, this wrestler by touching the socket of Jacob's thigh left him crippled as a continual reminder of the encounter. It may be this was the crucial experience Jacob referred to later when he confessed that the angel had redeemed him from all evil (Gen. 48:16). In the subsequent reconciliation, Jacob acknowledged God's gracious provision when he said to Esau, ". . . I see your face as one sees the face of God . . ." (33:10).

Arriving in Canaan, Jacob built an altar at Shechem, as Abraham before him had done, recognizing that his return was a fulfillment of God's promise (Gen. 33:20). When divinely instructed to move to Bethel and build an altar at this site where God had appeared to him en route to Mesopotamia, Jacob became keenly conscious of idolatry in his household. Exclusive devotion—the first stipulation essential in any suzerainty-vassal treaty in contemporary culture—was of primary importance in renewing his covenant with God. Consequently all idols were removed in preparation for meeting with God at Bethel, the place of God's initial revelation to Jacob.

At Bethel the patriarchal covenant was confirmed to Jacob. "God Almighty" assured royal nationhood to Jacob and his descendants in the land promised to Abraham and Isaac (35:-11–12).

Living in Canaan Jacob, who prior to his crucial experience at Peniel had been a deceiver, was subjected to fraud by his sons. When Joseph was sold by his brothers they led their father to believe that he had been eaten by wild beasts (Gen. 37). How much Jacob had shared with Joseph about the covenantal promise is not recorded. Joseph, however, reflected a God-consciousness throughout his life in Egypt that made that culture aware of the reality of God through his personal witness.

Serving as a slave in Potiphar's house, Joseph evaluated immorality as a "sin against God" (39:9). Subjected to prison after acting in harmony with his conviction, Joseph acknowledged in serving his fellow prisoners that the interpretation of dreams "belongs to God" (40:8). Subsequently, standing before Pharaoh to interpret his dreams, Joseph boldly asserts, "God has told Pharaoh what He is about to do" (41:25). When his brothers, due to the pressures of a famine in Canaan, are assembled before Joseph whom they now recognize as a powerful ruler in Egypt, he reveals his identity and interprets history for them. The simple facts are that they had sold him into Egypt but Joseph asserts that ". . . God sent me ahead of you to ensure that you will have descendants on earth. . . . it was not you who sent me here, but God. . . . he has made me ruler over all the land of Egypt . . ." (45:7–8).

Jacob found it difficult to believe that Joseph was still alive (45:26–28), but could hardly discount the evidence of wagons sent by Joseph to bring him to Egypt. En route at Beersheba, Jacob offered sacrifices to the "God of his father Isaac." At this occasion divine confirmation came to Jacob in his decision to take his whole family from the land of promise to the land of Egypt where Joseph made abundant provision for their welfare. By invitation and royal approval, Jacob and his sons settled in the fertile land of Goshen in the delta of the Nile.

For seventeen years Jacob saw his family prosper and multiply (57:27ff.). Anticipating that his time was limited, Jacob exacted a promise from Joseph concerning his own burial. He requested that he be buried in the cave of Machpelah where Abraham and Isaac had been interred.

Before his death Jacob made testamentary disposition, giving oral expression of blessings for his heirs (chaps. 48–49). He boldly affirmed that "God Almighty" had appeared to him in Canaan and had blessed him. Speaking prophetically, he assured them that God would be with them and bring them as a nation into the land of Canaan, designating Judah as the royal lineage.

The burial of Jacob gave witness to the covenant and must have made a unique impression upon the Israelite heirs as well as the Egyptians. The forty-day period of embalming and the seventy days of mourning for Jacob made the Egyptians aware of the death of a very important person, especially so since it was the father of Joseph who had successfully provided for Egypt through a severe famine. Among the Israelites, old and young were made conscious of the fact that they were heirs to the covenantal promises made to Abraham, Isaac, and Jacob as they fulfilled the dying request of Jacob to be buried in the cave of Machpelah in the land promised to all of them as a possession.

To Joseph was committed the guardianship of this covenantal promise. When Joseph died he was buried in Egypt. Before his death he exacted an oath from his sons that ultimately the bones of Joseph would be transferred to the land of Canaan. Joseph expressed the faith of his fathers when he assured his heirs that God would care for them and "bring you up from this land to the land which He promised on oath to Abraham, to Isaac, and to Jacob" (50:25).

IV

IN THE
BEGINNING

Abraham lived his life in the consciousness of the God of the universe. It was "the Lord, the God of heaven" who led him to Canaan (Gen. 24:7). Speaking to the king of Sodom, Abraham asserted with conviction that God was the creator or possessor of heaven and earth (14:22). Melchizedek, the king of Salem, may well have represented a community that recognized God as the "Maker of heaven and earth" (14:19). When Abraham exacted an oath from his servant, it was "by the Lord the God of heaven and the God of earth" (24:3). The knowledge Abraham had about God as creator and His relationship to the human race may have been based on the same account we have in these early chapters in Genesis.

A UNIQUE INTRODUCTION

Genesis 1–11 provides a unique introduction for the understanding of God, man, and the world in which man lives. A search in the areas of science, anthropology, archaeology, philosophy, or any other investigation into the past has not produced a more adequate solution to the questions of origins. As an introduction it stands unsurpassed.

Significant for Abraham's relationship with God was the fact that God was the maker of heaven above him and the earth in which he lived. What constituted heaven for Abraham was no more difficult to define or comprehend than it is for modern man. Heaven was the place from which he heard the voice of God. The vastness of the universe and even the extent of the earth beyond his local habitat was not as fully known to him as it is for man today. Whatever the limitations of his knowledge were, his relationship was by faith with the Maker of heaven and earth.

What did he know about God? God was in the beginning. God made heaven but beyond that fact not much information is given about it. God created the earth. On it order prevails. The sun, moon, and stars provide lumination for the earth with regularity so it can be productive to sustain life which God created for this world.

The ultimate questions that concern man are answered in this unique introduction. What is the ultimate power that animates the universe? What is life? What is man? How is man related to God, the universe, and the world about him?

To Abraham, God was the Maker of this universe and all that it contains. The opening chapter in Genesis delineates this simple yet profound truth: ". . . God created the heaven and the earth." Abraham, who was familiar with darkness and light, may not have grasped the significance as fully as modern man, who is more familiar with the relationship between energy and light and the splitting of the atom, when it says, "God divided," or separated, the light from the darkness.

Abraham was conscious of the stars in the heavens above him. This was the firmament, or expanse in which the sun and moon are seen and where the birds fly. Without realizing the vastness of this expanse and even contemplating man's ability to advance into outer space, he was aware of the simple truth that God made the firmament and called it heaven.

The land on which Abraham lived had been separated from the firmament above and the waters of the sea by God to provide sustenance for man. The luminaries—sun, moon, and stars

—God has ordained as servants to regulate day and night and the seasons for the earth's productivity.

Conscious life—living creatures in the sea below, birds in the firmament above, and living creatures on the earth—was created by God to abound and multiply. Climactic in God's work and activity was the creation of man.

"In the beginning" still offers the most adequate expression for dating creation in the distant past. It is unaltered by modern estimates that planet earth is about 4.6 billion years old as confirmed by dating of the rocks from the moon. When conscious life began or how long ago the Genesis man beginning with Adam lived on this earth is still an open question. If the Neanderthal man, dating back in the 40,000- to 70,000-year range, and the Cro-Magnon man appearing about 35,000 years ago are modern man, then the creation of Adam may be dated back to *ca.* 40,000 to 50,000 years.

Interestingly enough this Genesis introduction does not provide a chronology on which Abraham or modern man could establish the number of years back to Adam. The genealogical lists trace Abraham's lineage back to Noah (Gen. 10) and back to Adam (Gen. 5). When these records are compared with other genealogies in the rest of the Bible, it is apparent they were not written to be used for adding up chronological periods. The line of descent is given but generations may be omitted in lists, as is the case in Matthew, chapter 1, where the list of names can be checked with the kings as they are given in the books of Kings and Chronicles. Consequently Genesis 1–11 covers an extended period of time still open to investigation as to dating the creation of the universe, as well as the creation of man as he began his life on earth.

MAN—A UNIQUE CREATION

The account of the creation of the universe and all that is in it provides the essential background for the creation of man. Order and purpose emerge in a careful analysis indicating that

God and His creative works found culmination in the creation of man to whom everything was entrusted. Man created in the image of God was commissioned to

> be fruitful and multiply
> fill the earth
> subdue the earth
> rule over the fish of the sea
> > the birds of the sky
> > every living thing on the earth.

Everything that was made was "very good" according to the divine verdict (1:31).

Man was so important that he became the focal point beginning with Genesis 2:4. Whereas in the prologue God is related to the entire universe as Creator, in the rest of the introduction as well as the entire Bible the flow of history is concerned with the relationship between God and man.

Significant is the fact that more information is given concerning how God created man. Man was formed from the same source material—ground or dust of the ground—as the animals (cf. 2:7, 19). This inanimate dust-formation is animated by the breath of life and as a result becomes a "living creature" similar to and in the same classification, from the physical perspective, as the other "living creatures" which God had created (1:24; 2:19). The "breath of life" was common to all living creatures —man as well as animals (cf. 2:7; 6:17; 7:22). Significant is the fact that in God's creation, life was imparted directly to man as well as animals, both having been formed out of the ground.

That man was unique and distinct from the other "living creatures" God had created is clearly delineated in the context. Man was entrusted with God's creation to subdue the earth and fill it. He was endowed with ability to name the animals and birds and rule over them. Special mention is made of the creation of Eve, since man found no living creature suitable or corresponding to him. Adam and Eve had the ability and were given the responsibility to till the garden of Eden, which was prepared especially as their habitat. Above all, Adam and Eve were uniquely endowed with the capacity to communicate with God, setting them apart from all other creatures. Created in the image of God, man had the potential of relating to God in the capacity of being the recipient of divine revelation. The breaking and restoration of this relationship are crucial and pivotal developments.

Surrounded by an environment that expressed to them the love and care of their Creator, Adam and Eve were given the opportunity to enjoy everything that God had provided for them with one restriction—"not to eat of the tree of knowledge of good and evil" (2:17). They were subject to a very simple test in which all the involvements were explicitly delineated. They were confronted with a choice in their relationship with God: to obey, thereby showing their respect, reverence and love Godward for all He had provided, or to disobey, reflecting an attitude of knowing what was best for them.

The serpent represents more than an ordinary beast or living creature. The supernatural element is apparent in that the serpent is speaking. The fact emerges immediately that the one speaking is anti-God, and in subsequent Scriptures this speaker is identified as Satan (cf. Rev. 12:9; 20:2; and others). There is only one other incident in the Pentateuch where an animal speaks—God using a donkey to convey a message to Balaam (Num. 22:28). The serpent, representing the supernatural forces opposed to God, injects doubts as to what God has said and directly contradicts God's warning by assuring her "you surely shall not die" (3:4). Consider how Francis Schaeffer describes this crucial moment for Eve:

> The woman stands in her glory—the glory of being created in the image of God with no necessity upon her to choose evil. Standing in a perfect environment, having heard the voice of God, she is at a place where she can choose. What a wonder man is! Not

mechanical man, nor merely biological man, but man who can choose in a situation, as in the image of God, with no necessity upon him.

(Genesis in Space and Time, 1972; p. 80.)

The promise of being "like God" was enticing (3:5). Both Eve and Adam ate in direct disobedience to God who was their Creator and had provided for them as a loving father provides for his children. Through this choice they broke their relationship with God and were subjected to the drastic consequences. Adam and Eve immediately realized what they had done and sensed their guilt before God.

Mercy precedes judgment. Before Adam and Eve were expelled from Eden, a promise of redemption was given as God announced doom upon the tempter. The allegiance of the tempter would be reversed in the enmity that would exist between the two parties. In the ensuing struggle victory was assured to the woman's offspring who would bruise the head of the serpent. The fatality of the party whose head is crushed stands in contrast to the bruising of the heel of the woman's seed. This assurance of victory provided a basis for hope and an opportunity for faith in God to fulfill His promise. Ostracized from the garden, Eve was subjected to the prospects of suffering in childbearing but in the hope of a victor through her seed. Because of Adam's sin, the ground became a power reclaiming man in death.

Very little is recorded about the increase in the first family. In view of the hope that Eve expressed when Cain was born, it is very significant to note the relationship that developed between him and his brother Abel born later. Both were conscious of their need to acknowledge God by bringing offerings —Cain bringing farm produce while Abel offered a lamb. When Cain responded with anger because his offering was not acceptable, he was divinely warned. Cain acted against better knowledge in killing Abel, his brother. Very likely God had revealed the need for a blood sacrifice—possibly through Adam and Eve when He provided skins for their covering, implying the killing of an animal as a substitute for them. The fact that Cain acted against better knowledge when God warned him may indicate that he had done this previously in bringing an offering of his own choice. Cain and his descendants subsequently reflected this in their culture in an attitude of alienation from God where polygamy and vengeful tyranny prevailed through generation after generation.

New hope came to Adam and Eve in the birth of Seth (4:25). In this lineage there was some favorable response to God. Notable as God-fearing persons were Enoch and Noah. With the birth of Noah special mention is made of the hope that through him they would be redeemed from the curse under which they were suffering (5:29).

With the passing of centuries, possibly millenniums of time, the civilization man had developed was permeated with an attitude of disregard for God who had entrusted man with dominion over the earth. "The sons of the gods" (6:2)—perhaps a better translation, since kings were so identified in ancient literature—and the "Nephilim" or "mighty men," which may reflect giant stature but perhaps more adequately political dominance, seemed to rule and reign, exercising their power without regard for God or the rights of their fellow citizens. This was especially apparent in their polygamous practices. Failure to respect, acknowledge, and love God resulted in mistreatment of their fellow man on earth. The total situation is described as follows:

> Man had done much evil on earth
> The whole bent of his thinking produced nothing but
>   evil continually (6:5).
>
> The whole earth was corrupt before God
> The earth was filled with injustice
> God saw the corruption

> All men lived corrupt lives on the earth
> The earth was filled with violence because of man (6:11–13).

Judgment was preceded by mercy as a 120–year period of grace was announced. Noah, who was a righteous and blameless man, adjusted his pattern of living habitually Godward. In obedience to divine instructions, Noah built the ark.

God established a covenant with Noah. He and those who entered with him were sustained in the ark while divine judgment came upon all mankind. The terminal point of God's mercy extended to the human race was set by God when He shut the door (7:16), separating the remnant that was saved from the rest of mankind that perished in the flood. This covenant promise of mercy for Noah in time of universal judgment was fulfilled in the coming of the flood.

The flood was a catastrophic judgment uniquely outstanding between man's expulsion from Eden and the final consummation awaiting this world. That it affected the entire human race is clearly delineated in the divine purpose, whether the flood was universal or limited. How much this supernatural event affected the uniformity of a simple cause-and-effect line may never be fully ascertained from man's limited perspective of the millenniums of the past.

Noah acknowledged God in worship after leaving the ark. He built an altar and offered burnt offerings to God. The judgment upon the human race had involved the earth so that a year had passed without seedtime and harvest. God's promise in response to Noah's sacrifice was that never again would a curse be sent upon this earth because of man. Seasons and days would not be disrupted again so that seedtime and harvest would continue with regularity as long as the earth remains (Gen. 8:20–22).

God's relationship with the human race is delineated in a covenant (9:1–17). The responsibility given previously to Adam is repeated in the command to fill or populate the earth, to exercise dominion over every living creature, and to use the produce of the earth as nourishment for all living creatures—man as well as animals, birds, and sea life. Additional are the instructions that all living creatures, excepting man, are to be used as food to sustain man with the explicit prohibition regarding the sanctity of blood, which was related to life itself.

Man was responsible for government, or man's relationship with his fellow man. God instructed man to take the life of any man who committed murder. Man was given permission to kill any living creature except man because living-creature-man was created in the image of God. Man was commanded to execute the man who was guilty of disregarding God's command that man should not take the life of another man. Man's attitude toward God determined his attitude toward his neighbor. It was the God-fearing person who had the responsibility to administer justice in the death of a killer (9:5–6).

God's covenant was universal. Note the threefold aspect of universality. To Noah and his descendants—the entire human race—God made this commitment. Involved also were all the other living creatures in sea, earth, and sky. The earth, which God had created as man's domain to sustain life of all living creatures, would never again be subjected to a catastrophic flood.

God's covenant was everlasting. It would be sustained as long as the earth endures.

God's covenant was unconditional. It did not depend on man's obedience, since the "intent of man's heart is evil from his youth" (8:21). God promised to keep His commitment even though man failed in his.

The sign of the covenant was the bow in the sky. The rainbow may or may not have been apparent earlier, but for Noah and all his descendants throughout coming generations the bow in the sky would signify God's promise that

> I will remember My covenant, which is between Me and you and every living creature of all flesh; and never again shall the water become a flood to destroy all flesh (9:15).

The rainbow in the sky was given as the recurring sign in the heavens above that God remembers His promise to man who is made in His image, to all other creatures, and to the earth. God repeatedly gives the assurance that

> While the earth remains,
> Seedtime and harvest,
> And cold and heat,
> And summer and winter,
> And day and night
> Shall not cease (8:22).

The flow of history from Noah to Abraham is delineated summarily through the genealogical lineage given in Genesis, chapter 11, even as the era from Adam to Noah was summarized in chapter 5. Since these genealogies do not offer guidance for dating—at least biblical writers nowhere use them as giving an estimate of time—it is reasonable to consider the anthropological studies on dating this period and think in terms of the flood occurring in the 20,000 to 10,000 B.C. era. Any approximations of dates in this early period should be held tentatively and are open to further modification.

What the God-man relationship was during this long period and what was divinely revealed to supplement previous revelation is briefly indicated. God's initial provision displaying His love and mercy by entrusting to man the garden of Eden was forfeited by Adam and Eve through disobedience. When Cain defied God and murdered Abel, a divine curse was pronounced upon him (4:11). When subsequent generations gave way to godlessness, divine judgment came upon the entire race, with only Noah's family being preserved alive through the flood.

Concurrent with the curse announced in the garden was the promise of hope and restoration. Although Adam and Eve and all their descendants were subjected to the consequences of the curse, the assurance was given that in the struggle throughout succeeding generations there would emerge a victor in the lineage of man defeating the serpent, or Satan. Hope that God would fulfill this promise was expressed in the birth of Cain (4:1), the birth of Seth (4:25), and the birth of Noah (5:29).

Two crucial events are recorded that indicate God's relationship with Noah and his descendants to whom divine assurance was given that they would not be destroyed by a catastrophic flood. The divine-human relationship is reflected in Noah's pronouncement concerning the future, and the divine judgment upon human pride manifested in the building of the tower of Babel.

Noah began farming after the flood by planting a vineyard. Yielding to intemperance in the drinking of wine, he became drunk, which precipitated indecent exposure as he lay naked in his tent. When Ham, probably accompanied by his son Canaan, came upon this unfortunate scene, he apparently took delight in telling his two brothers about the state of Noah. Shem and Japheth by contrast showed respect for their father by immediately providing a covering for him.

Nakedness for Adam and Eve became indecent exposure after their act of disobedience in the garden. Sensing their guilt, they tried to hide from God by making themselves loin coverings from fig leaves. To alleviate this sense of shame and guilt, God provided garments of skin to clothe man. The circumstance of Noah's sin of drunkenness and nakedness precipitated the attitude and action which provided the framework for a curse upon Canaan and a blessing upon Shem and Japheth. Both are precipitated by this crisis.

On this occasion Noah foresees the curse operative in Canaan's lineage. The lowest of servants was to be his lot in serving his brothers. Canaan was the progenitor of the Canaanites who were later displaced by the Israelites in their occupation of the land of Canaan. Shem, or the Semites, will be blessed in a vital relationship with God so that the Japhethites will look to them to share as beneficiaries of God's favor. In spite of the depravity of some of his offspring, Noah predicts that blessing will come through Shem, possibly anticipating the fulfillment of the victory promised through the seed of Eve.

The building of the tower of Babel created a crisis in divine-human relationship precipitating a judgment that affected the whole human race permanently. This effort was the "first public declaration of humanism" (Schaeffer, *op. cit.*, p. 152) and represented a display of human pride.

The Genesis narrative bears all the marks of a reliable historical account of the constructions of buildings even though these buildings have not yet been identified. The construction of staged towers known as ziggurats developed in the third millennium B.C. in Babylonia. With a central shrine on a structure equivalent to a mountain surrounded by business centers and houses, the Chalcolithic period people created a sense of community with an immanent god represented among them. Ziggurats identified at Babylon and the staged tower at Borsippa seven miles south date to the Neo-Babylonian era (*ca.* 600 B.C.). The tower at Dur-Kurigalzu, west of Baghdad, possibly dates back to 1400 B.C. It is quite likely that the tower of Babel may never be identified because of its antiquity.

The purpose of the Babel builders was

> to build a city for ourselves
> to build a tower reaching to the skies
> to make ourselves famous
> to avoid dispersion over all the earth (11:4).

This effort as a whole represented a mounting human arrogance and the blatant embodiment of an ungodly spirit. By their plan and action they defied the divine word to them to dominate and populate the earth. Instead of worshiping and acknowledging their Creator, they gave way to lust for a name to maintain human unity and social stability in a humanistic culture.

Divine judgment came in the dispersion of the race through the confusion of their language. The communication breakdown not only frustrated their building efforts but resulted in their dispersion.

Babel meant "gate-of-god" according to popular etymology in the Sumerian and Babylonian renderings. In the Genesis narrative the satirical polemic is expressed in the Babel-*balal* pun as "confusion" or "mixing." In English the name Babylon for Babel is based on the Greek *Babylon*. Reflecting this Mosaic account, Babel has become a synonym for the confusion that resulted from the linguistic differences divinely initiated to terminate the building of a tower which displayed the pride of man.

From the human perspective the dispersion of the race seemed like a curse. Man was frustrated in his autonomous ambitions of human progress. Now people willingly scattered as God had commanded Noah and his descendants to populate the earth so that iniquity, which accompanied the progress of man's civilization, was retarded temporarily.

The Genesis introduction (chaps. 1–11) concludes with a selective genealogy from Noah to Abraham accounting for the dispersion of the human race as it unfolded in the flow of history during this long period of time. In the lineage of Shem, through whom Noah anticipated that the divine-human relationship would be continued, the history narrows down to the individual Abraham who responds to the call of God and through whom divine blessing ultimately comes to all the nations of the earth.

V

THE PENTATEUCH AND
MODERN SCHOLARSHIP

Why do college and seminary textbooks, commentaries, Bible dictionaries, Bibles with study helps, and Christian education curriculums regard the Pentateuch as composed of legends, myths, folk tales, fiction, and folklores? Why do they represent Moses as leading only a few of the twelve tribes from Egypt through the desert? Why do they consider the tabernacle and the priesthood associated with Israel in the Pentateuch as a figment of the imagination?

The popular view that the Pentateuch is composed of documents written beginning in the ninth century B.C. and completed by about 400 B.C. provides the basis for these perspectives. The dating of the composition of the first five books of the Bible basically affects and often determines the interpretation of the content. That the theory of authorship provides the framework for interpretation is willingly acknowledged by authors of textbooks offering an interpretation of the Old Testament. (Cf. R. H. Pfeiffer *Old Testament Introduction*, 1941; p. 141; Gerald Larue, *Old Testament Life and Literature*, pp. 31–33; and others).

The viewpoint that Moses was responsible for the Pentateuch as held by Jewish and Christian scholars was brought into question during the eighteenth century. The literary partition of

Genesis was suggested by Witter (1711) and Astruc (1753) on the basis of two names used for deity in the first two chapters. Eichhorn (1775) developed this idea of documents on a scientific basis, identifying literary styles for various documents throughout the entire Pentateuch. Graf (1865) advocated the theory that the laws during Old Testament times developed from the simple to the complex. The classic exposition of this documentary hypothesis in contrast to Mosaic authorship was published by Julius Wellhausen (1878). Using the literary analysis with ingenuity and creativity he proposed four hypothetical documents, each reflecting the times in which they were written—J (Jehovah) composed during Jehoshaphat's reign, *ca.* 850 B.C.; E (Elohim) written during the time of Jeroboam II, *ca.* 750 B.C.; D (Deuteronomy) originating during the Josian era, ca. 650 B.C.; and P (Priestly Code) dated in exilic times, *ca.* 550 B.C.— for the composition of the Pentateuch by about 400 B.C. Wellhausen was influenced by Hegel and Darwin in advocating the concept that Israel's religion evolved from animism to national henotheism and finally under the influence of the prophets and exilic conditions into ethical monotheism. The book of Genesis yielded no historical knowledge. The patriarchs were but primitive nomads and the religion of Israel began with the exodus. The law came in the wake of the prophetic movement which began in the eighth century, while the psalms were largely exilic or later.

The Wellhausen position regarding the composition of the Pentateuch seemed so reasonable, sure, and satisfying to contemporary scholarship that it gained a wide acceptance. Penetratingly influential in the dissemination of this theory was the book by S. R. Driver, *Introduction to the Literature of the Old Testament,* published in 1891 and republished in the Meridian series in 1957. During the early decades of this century many volumes in Old Testament studies were published, not the least of which was *Introduction to the Old Testament* by R. H. Pfeiffer in 1941. Optimism prevailed that this literary-critical method had produced results that were firmly established and assured for all times.

Although confessing adherence to the Wellhausen theory, Hermann Gunkel (1901) developed the school of form criticism through his research into the life situations in which the religious ideas in the folklore of Genesis had their origin. This concentration on the origin and growth of early sources developed into a fundamental criticism and brought about a reaction to the Wellhausen scheme. Scandinavian scholars stressed oral tradition as the means by which the Pentateuchal material was transmitted from generation to generation until the Jews in exilic times composed the Pentateuch. In essence these scholars abandoned the Wellhausen theory of datable documents before exilic times and considered the existence of a redactor who combined these documents as pleasant fiction.

The vast resources of archaeology made available since the turn of the century have revolutionized the attitude of many scholars toward biblical historical traditions and made a decided impact upon scholarship in questioning the two basic tenets of the Wellhausen theory. Outstanding among linguists and archaeologists, William Foxwell Albright through his innumerable contributions in the entire field of ancient oriental history has exerted an influence in Old Testament studies unequaled in current times. His impact through publications and stimulating scholarship in classroom and public lectures contributed toward bringing Old Testament criticism into a state of flux so that adjustments to new data and new insights became imperative. In appraising the contemporary attitude in Old Testament studies, John Bright in 1959 asserted that "few are left today who would find a melioristic evolution a sufficient explanation of human history—and, by the same token, of Israel's history. Deprived of its philosophical rationale, the critical structure was left vulnerable." In the same year, however, H. H. Rowley in the Peake memorial lectures asserted that in common with the majority of scholars he still accepted Wellhausen's view of the origin of the Pentateuch.

That the documentary hypothesis of Pentateuchal authorship advocated by Wellhausen has been modified is apparent in recent publications. Whereas the theory of the evolution of Israel's religion has been largely abandoned, the essential idea that the Pentateuch was completed in exilic times with basic documents developed during the kingdom era is still the framework or basis for the interpretation of the Pentateuch and the rest of the Old Testament. Discussing his analysis of the Pentateuch, G. A. Larue in his *Old Testament Life and Literature* (1968; p. 31) writes:

> Most present-day scholarship accepts the basic premises of the documentary hypothesis—namely, that different source materials are to be found, that the labels J, E, D, P, are acceptable for major sources, and that the order of development is that proposed in the Graf-Wellhausen thesis.

Subsequently (p. 33) he states his perspective in interpreting the Pentateuch: "Because the documentary hypothesis is the most widely accepted of all theories of Pentateuchal analysis, this book will utilize, in principle, the conclusions reached by this method of research." By way of modification he dates the J and E documents both in the tenth century, whereas Wellhausen dated them respectively in the ninth and eighth.

H. K. Beebe reflects the same position in *The Old Testament* published in 1970 asserting: "even though some scholars have questioned the accuracy of the Documentary Hypothesis, it still functions as an effective tool in discovering the origins of Israel" (p. 122). He indicates how Wellhausen's documentary hypothesis has been improved, first, in the recognition "that oral tradition continued to flow even after literary works were composed," and second, that "the creative genius of authorship is clearly visible in three documents. It is no longer possible to think of the authors of J, E, and P as mere collectors of Israelite traditions. J, at least, put the seal on Hebrew literature so as to influence all subsequent narrative styles" (p. 121).

Based upon the theoretical presuppositions and methodological speculations of Old Testament scholarship, interpretations of the Pentateuch represented in the above examples continue to be published in current commentaries, textbooks, and Bible study helps. Even though the evidence and arguments for the Wellhausen theories with its a priori speculations have been called into question, the documentary hypothesis—in its modified and improved form—advocating a late composition of the Pentateuch is still used as a basic perspective for Old Testament interpretation. What J. Kaufmann observed in 1960 in *The Religion of Israel* seems to be applicable in part currently, "Yet biblical scholarship, while admitting that the grounds have crumbled away, nevertheless continues to adhere to the conclusions. . . . Equally unable to accept the theory in its classical formulation and to return to the precritical views of tradition, biblical scholarship has entered upon a period of search for new foundations."

PRECRITICAL VIEW

What can be said for the precritical view of the Pentateuch associating Moses personally with the events recorded in Exodus–Deuteronomy and considering Genesis as the normative background transmitted to Moses from his ancestors? Has twentieth-century scholarship provided new data and insights supporting this point of view?

Scholarship and research have led some scholars of the highest caliber to ascertain to the best of their ability the actual facts about the cultural life prevailing in the ancient Near East during Old Testament times. Allowing criticism to be based upon the assured foundation of life situations in the Near East, they have recognized that the early date of the Pentateuch has more support than the occidental philosophical or methodological speculations which are the basis for a late-date composition of the Pentateuch. Representative of this position, R. K. Harrison in his *Introduction to the Old Testament* (1969; p. 541) asserts, "In the view of the present writer, almost the entire body of Pentateuchal material could have been easily extant in practically its present form by the late Joshua period." Allowing for some linguistic and editorial changes in the course of subsequent centuries he continues, ". . . there appears to be no substantial ground for denying that the Pentateuch in virtually its extant form was in existence by the time of Samuel."

Kenneth A. Kitchen in his volume *Ancient Orient and Old Testament* (1966) states in his preface that he intends "to give some idea of the kind of contribution that Ancient Near Eastern studies can make to the study of the Old Testament, and towards a critical reassessment of problems and methods in the Old Testament field." After discussing problems in the Old Testament with a major emphasis on the Pentateuch and suggesting solutions he concludes (p. 172):

> It is solely because the data from the Ancient Near East coincide so much better with the existing observable structure of Old Testament history, literature and religion than with the theoretical reconstructions, that we are compelled—as happens in Ancient Oriental studies—to question or even to abandon such theories regardless of their popularity. Facts not votes determine the truth. We do not merely advocate a return to "pre-critical" views and traditions (e.g., of authorship) merely for their own sake or for the sake of theological orthodoxy. Let it be clearly noted that *no appeal whatsoever* has been made to any theological starting-point in the body of this work, not to mention the miasma of late post-biblical Jewish or patristic (or later) Christian traditions. If some of the results reached here approximate to a traditional view or seem to agree with theological orthodoxy, then this is simply because the tradition in question or that orthodoxy are that much closer to the real facts than is commonly realized. While one must indeed never prefer mere orthodoxy

to truth, it is also perverse to deny that orthodox views can be true.

The interpretation of the Pentateuch from the perspective of its internal claims reflecting the time of Moses has much in its favor when serious and honest consideration is given to the contemporary culture of the Near East. It is not the purpose of the present writer to offer an exhaustive study in this volume but merely to provide some insight and refer the reader to some who have entered into extensive research in these matters.

The book of Deuteronomy has been quite widely recognized as a clear example of ancient suzerainty treaties in numerous recent studies. More limited is the acknowledgment that Deuteronomy is better identified with the late second millennium treaties as asserted by K. Kitchen (*op. cit.*, pp. 92–98) than with the later treaties of the first millennium B.C. In his volume *Treaty of the Great King*, which includes a commentary on Deuteronomy, Meredith Kline delineates his analysis of Deuteronomy as a treaty between God and Israel. His basic outline reprinted in his more recent publication *The Structure of Biblical Authority* (1972) with the references in Deuteronomy according to the standard treaty pattern is as follows:

> Preamble   1:1–5
> Historical Prologue   1:6–4:49
> Stipulations   5–26
> Curses and Blessings or Covenant Ratification   27–30
> Succession Arrangements or Covenant Continuity   31–34

Kitchen in his comparative analysis points out that the patterns of earlier treaties were more elaborate and the treaties of the first millennium were much less extensive, whereas the pattern of second-millennium treaties and the book of Deuteronomy have the greatest similarity in common.

As a literary unit the book of Deuteronomy claims to be a renewal of the Sinaitic covenant by Moses to Israel through which he transferred the leadership to Joshua. If this claim is taken seriously, then this Deuteronomic treaty was produced for this particular occasion when Joshua was installed as leader —similar to other contemporary treaties drawn up specifically for an occasion involving dynastic succession—and not developed by gradual accretion and growth, reaching its final form by about 400 B.C. The gradual-growth viewpoint for the composition of Deuteronomy reduces to fiction as portrayed by a later writer the idea that Moses gave a farewell speech and that Joshua was appointed as leader.

The question of predictive prophecy becomes a basic issue in interpretation if the claims of Deuteronomy are taken at face value. If a scholar adopts the naturalistic presupposition that there is no predictive prophecy in the Old Testament—a view held by R. H. Pfeiffer of Harvard, Gerhard von Rad, and others —then all that Moses said about Israel concerning the immediate and distant future was written later when these matters such as the exile could be recorded as history. On the other hand, if Moses is recognized as a prophet through whom divine revelation came to Israel, then predictive prophecy becomes normative as represented in the book of Deuteronomy.

THE HISTORIC REVELATION

If the book of Deuteronomy is taken realistically as a historical renewal of the covenant, then the formulation of the original covenant comes into serious consideration. Can the account as given in Exodus be correlated with the situation as it existed in the classic age of treaty diplomacy in the third quarter of the second millennium in the ancient Near East?

The covenant established between God and Israel stands at the heart of Israel's religion. George E. Mendenhall in his notable volume *Law and Covenant in Israel and the Ancient Near East* (1955) points out that striking parallels exist between this covenant (Exod. 20ff.) and the international treaties of the fourteenth/thirteenth centuries B.C. Upon examination of further evidence K. A. Kitchen confirms this in his analysis in *Ancient Orient and Old Testament,* (1966; pp. 92–102).

Certain aspects common to the formulation of the Sinaitic covenant and ancient Near Eastern treaties of the time of Moses are significant for the interpretation of the Old Testament and especially the Pentateuch. Significantly pertinent is the discussion of Meredith Kline in his recent publication *The Structure of Biblical Authority* (1972; pp. 27–44).

The Sinaitic covenant like ancient treaties was given to Israel in written form. Writing was common to the Near East in the Mosaic age with evidence of cylinder inscriptions dating back into the fourth millennium B.C. In some treaties the suzerain asserted that he himself wrote the agreement on tablets. Usually these tablets were in duplicate form so that they were deposited respectively in the presence of the god of the suzerain and the god of the vassal. For the Israelites both copies were deposited in the ark of the covenant in the tabernacle.

The covenant at Sinai also was authoritative. In this respect it was similar to the authority of the suzerain who made the terms of the treaty for his vassal to accept. This authority is reflected in the broader perspectives of Near Eastern treaties or documents where sometimes a curse is pronounced upon anyone who tried to alter or destroy such agreements. The authority in these treaties was not vested in the vassal, nor in community approval, but issued out of the will of the suzerain. The covenant at Mount Sinai was authoritative because it was divinely revealed and thus had its origin with God.

This written authoritative document or covenant was thus carefully guarded and available to the community for public reading. In this way the terms of the covenant were disseminated orally to the populace at large from the written copy.

This historic event of the giving of the covenant by God to Israel marks the birth of the Old Testament canon. At Sinai Israel was established as a nation, as God's kingdom of priests or God's holy people (Exod. 19:5). The instrument was a written, God-given document, similar to contemporary treaties, which provided guidance for them to live as God's kingdom people. This document was authoritative because it was God-breathed and not because they declared it to be authoritative.

That this covenant marked the historic beginning in a written document that had authority through divine revelation is determinative concerning the canonicity of the Pentateuch. The canon concept traditionally held by Jews and Christians was inherent in this nuclear Old Testament. Divine revelation and inspiration were directly involved in the written document establishing the covenant relationship between God and Israel.

In contrast to this view is the theory that the Pentateuch was completed and adopted as authoritative by the Jewish community by about 400 B.C. Representative of this perspective is Norman Gottwald who states in his volume *A Light to the Nations* (1959; p. 30): "The promulgation of the book of Deuteronomy as the law of Judah by Josiah in 621 B.C. marked the first time in Hebrew history that a particular book became authoritative." He suggests that in time the records of God's revelation were recognized as revelation and on the basis of religious usage the first stage of canonization occurred in which "the Law, containing the basic revelation to Moses, was given authority around 400–350 B.C."

In *The Old Testament* (1970) H. K. Beebe states, "The idea of divine revelation as given through certain special men was formulated into doctrine, however, when the book of Deuteronomy was canonized," basing his interpretation on II Kings 22–23. Concerning the Pentateuch he continues, "In subsequent generations, Judaism gave sacred status to the first five books of the Old Testament when the three epic narratives and the ancient laws had been formulated into a single work and the scroll of Deuteronomy associated with them" (p. 13). The scrolls composing the Pentateuch, or Torah, then became "canon" about 400 B.C.

Representative of current literature used in teaching and interpreting the Old Testament, Jay G. Williams in *Understanding the Old Testament* (1972; p. 10) candidly states, "We know little about the early formation of the Hebrew canon, but most scholars agree that the first part of it, i.e., the Pentateuch or *Torah,* gained official authoritative status about 400 B.C."

The crucial question concerning the authoritative status of the Pentateuch is one of human judgment versus divine origin. Is the Pentateuch authoritative because a community or council *declared* it to be so on the basis of their judgment or because they *recognized* that it had divine authority having its origin in God? If the Pentateuch is taken seriously as a reliable record of what actually happened, then this recognition of authority in a written covenant given through Moses began with Israel at Mount Sinai and is reflected throughout the rest of the Pentateuch, Joshua, and the rest of the Old Testament. In comparing this with contemporary Near Eastern treaties, numerous scholars have come to consider that similar recognition of authority was common in that culture and that the biblical perspective is in accord with the facts of history. The theory that canonization began with Deuteronomy in Josian times and culminated in the Jewish community giving divine authority to the Pentateuch by about 400 B.C. seems to be directly related to the late-date composition theory and so far lacks historical support.

ISRAELITE LAWS

Are the laws in the Pentateuch properly identified as codes of law? Is the Pentateuch at heart legalistic? How does the legal material associated with Moses compare with the contemporary law collections in the ancient Near East? How do the laws in the Pentateuch relate to the covenant relationship established between God and Israel at Mount Sinai?

The hypothesis propagated by Graf and Wellhausen that the law in Israel came after the eighth-century prophets has been abandoned as archaeological advance has shed further light on the Near Eastern culture of the second millennium B.C. Since the turn of the century, four law collections have been discovered that predate the time of Moses: the Sumerian laws of Ur-Nammu, who was king in the Third Dynasty of Ur about 2050 B.C.; the Akkadian laws of Bilalama, who was king of Eshnunna about 1900 B.C.; the law collection of Lipit-Ishtar, king of Isin about 1868 B.C.; and the most extensive and best-known collection of Hammurabi, the famous king of Babylon about 1700 B.C. In the light of these discoveries it has seemed more reasonable from the naturalistic perspective to recognize laws for Israel in the second millennium B.C.

Although the word "code" is commonly used in designating the Near Eastern law collections mentioned above as well as the biblical laws, it is somewhat misleading against the background of Napoleonic and Roman codes of law. Contending that the very concept of law needs to be interpreted against an oriental background Harrison (*op. cit.*, p. 535) writes, "Even in Mesopotamia, where codified law was an early and familiar concept, the law-courts did not cite the codes in handing down decisions, but instead functioned in accordance with custom, precedent, and accepted tradition, a point that still has not been grasped by occidental scholars." Favoring the abandonment of the word "code," Kitchen suggests that "law-collection," "laws," or "legal usage" is a more appropriate way of identifying the Mesopotamian and biblical laws of this early period.

When the setting for Old Testament laws contained in documentary units like the Ten Commandments and Deuteronomy are given serious consideration as given in the Pentateuch, it is obvious that these law collections are treaty stipulations. With keen insight Kline (*op. cit.*, p. 48) observes, "But the other Pentateuchal laws are also set in a covenantal context. This context may be rejected as secondary in modern subjective reconstructions, but in the objective Pentateuchal setting in which they come to us these laws are presented as elaborations of the treaty obligations laid upon Israel as Yahweh continued to speak to them through the covenant mediator Moses."

When the laws in the Pentateuch are recognized as treaty stipulations issuing out of God-Israel relationship initiated and established by God, the uniqueness of this law collection emerges in a comparison with laws in contemporary cultures. Although given in the pattern of man-with-man treaties—which had sacred sanction by involving the gods of the suzerain and the vassal respectively—Israel's treaty was a God-man covenant. Consequently many laws which were matters of state elsewhere were cultus-absorbed features of covenantal administration in Israel. For the Israelites the whole pattern of living came under the regulations of God's covenant with them, and the wide varieties of laws reflected God's comprehensive interest and claim in all areas and dimensions of life.

Israelite laws as a whole had a kind and humane character when compared with contemporary collections. In the Hammurabi code the emphasis was first upon procedure, then property, and third upon persons. Biblical laws considered persons most important, emphasizing the rights of the common man. In matters of theft the former often required the death penalty whereas the latter insisted upon restitution of property. In Israel slaves were to be treated decently and could become part of an Israelite family. In Mesopotamian laws, high interest rates could be collected but in Israel these were prohibited.

Although the general principle prevailed in secular treaties that a vassal was to be a friend to the suzerain's friend and an enemy to his enemies, the Israelite stipulations reflected the fact that the foundation of their laws was the covenant. Their vertical relationship with God determined their horizontal relationship with man. They were to be kind to the poor because God was the avenger of the oppressed. God had delivered them from Egyptian bondage, therefore they were to be kind and show love for the servant, the foreigner, and the oppressed. Love for man issued out of their relationship with a righteous and merciful God (Lev. 19:18; Deut. 10:12–22).

MOSES AND GENESIS

Was the book of Genesis written by an editor who used various documents and oral tradition shortly before the Pentateuch was completed by about 400 B.C., as held by the documentary hypothesis? Does our present knowledge of ancient Near East literary activity during the second millennium B.C. provide a basis for assigning the compilation of the book of Genesis to the time of Moses?

In his recent examination of these questions, R. K. Harrison (*op.cit.*, pp. 542–65) brings into focus the practice of Near Eastern scribes as indicated on the cuneiform tablets from this early period. Often the first line was used as the title or catch-line for identifying a tablet. After the body of the text they frequently used a colophon which, among other things, might identify the scribe or the owner, a cylinder seal, and sometimes a date. The colophon would serve as a distinctive feature for identification, especially if there were a series of tablets. Authorship frequently was anonymous.

That the book of Genesis has a distinguishing phrase in the expression, "These are the generations of," has been widely recognized by scholars for quite some time. A careful examination of the usage seems to indicate that this expression is not the preface or introduction to a literary unit—as scholars like S. R. Driver and others have held—but is the conclusion to a chronicle of events sometimes including genealogies that occurred during the lives of the individuals mentioned. The Hebrew word translated "generation" means "history," "narrative," or "genealogical record." Each literary unit which concluded with this expression seems to describe family origins, with the introductory unit telling about the origin of the heaven and the earth (1:1–2:4).

Considering the expression "These are the generations of" to be the key to the book of Genesis, Harrison, following P. J. Wiseman (*New Discoveries in Babylonia about Genesis,* 1958;

p. 3), asserts that the eleven literary units in chapters 1–36 are "a series of tablets whose contents were linked together to form a roughly chronological account of primeval and patriarchal life written from the standpoint of a Mesopotamian cultural milieu." In all units except the first two, all events recorded could have been known to the person mentioned so that this material may represent genuine literary sources available to Moses in cuneiform tablets.

The Joseph narrative in chapters 37–50 according to Harrison may have been in "oral form when Moses was alive, and it may be that it was he who reduced it to writing in magnificent literary Hebrew."

ORAL TRADITION AND WRITTEN SOURCES

That oral tradition may have been the basis for Moses in composing the Joseph account in Genesis seems reasonable in the cultural context of his time. That the Pentateuch as a whole rests upon oral tradition prior to Davidic times, after which documents are written that in subsequent centuries are gradually combined with continuing oral tradition to form one literary unit, is open to serious questions on factual and methodological grounds.

Could Moses write? The Wellhausen dictum that Moses could not possibly have written the Pentateuch was advocated as late as 1893 (cf. H. Schultz, *Old Testament Theology*, I, p. 25). This assumption was based on the theory that writing before Davidic times was uncommon and limited to the specialists.

The prominent place of the written word throughout the ancient Near East is evident through the mass of cuneiform tablets, ostraca, and papyri that have been uncovered. Trained scribes could be drawn from any class, and most higher administrative officials were literate. Interesting and pertinent is the fact that the city of Alalakh in Syria with a population of about two thousand had six scribes *ca.* 1800–1500 B.C. D. J. Wiseman points out that "recent studies show that scribes may have learned their Akkadian at main 'university' centers such as Aleppo in Syria or Babylon itself" (cf. "Writing" in *The New Bible Dictionary,* p. 1351). At least five scripts were in use during this period: Egyptian hieroglyphs, Sinaitic pictographs, Byblian alphabet, Akkadian cuneiform, and the Ugaritic alphabetic cuneiform. These were in use in the biblical world of the patriarchs and Israel extending throughout the fertile crescent from the Persian Gulf through Palestine down into Egypt.

How important was written material in the ancient Near East? What was the relationship between written material and oral tradition? How was material valuable to coming generations passed on to them?

On the basis of what is currently known about the life situations prevailing in the Near East, Kenneth A. Kitchen makes the following observation (*Ancient Orient and Old Testament,* p. 136):

> For transmission of anything important to posterity, the Ancient Orient insistently resorted to written rather than oral transmission. This is sufficiently illustrated by the hundreds of thousands of clay tablets from Mesopotamia and the acres of hieroglyphic texts and scenes from Egypt covering all aspects of life. The pompous annals of energetic kings and the cuneiform litigation or humble hieroglyphic stelae of citizens of very modest means alike show that neither national traditions nor the repute of individuals was left to the care of campfire bards in the Ancient Near East.

Oral transmission was commonly used to disseminate information from the written copy to the populace at large, since methods of duplicating written materials for mass distribution were unknown. To interpret oral tradition as applying to transmission of important material from generation to generation seems to be unwarranted, since the uniform testimony of oriental literary practice demanded that matters important for posterity were committed to writing and not left to campfire romancers.

This misinterpretation of the use of oral tradition is used to account for cult legends, myths, traditions concerning the patriarchs and Israel under Moses' leadership, and laws that may date back to pre-Davidic times for the late-date composition of the Pentateuch. Representative of the position that Moses would not have written the Pentateuch, Norman Gottwald (*A Light to the Nations,* p. 103) asserts, "One of the certain results of modern Bible study has been the discovery that the first five books of the Old Testament were not written by Moses." In stating the tentative position for the composition of the Pentateuch, the oral sources are of primary importance and diminish as written sources are developed by writers and editors throughout the centuries culminating in one literary unit by about 400 B.C.

When the Pentateuch is taken seriously against the background of ancient Near Eastern culture as it has become known in recent times, it is reasonable to consider Moses as its author. Being trained in Egypt when the pharaohs extended their control up to the Euphrates River, Moses may have had as classmates royal hostages from the city-states in Palestine and Syria so that the culture and languages of the fertile crescent became part of his general education. His awareness of the divine promises to the patriarchs and his involvement in leading the Israelites out of Egypt to the land of Canaan provided the general circumstances in which he would have been concerned to write an account of God's relationship with man available to posterity. The book of Genesis provided the introduction and background as Moses reminded the Israelites on the Moab plains that God's love for them as a chosen people began with the patriarchs.

The covenant between God and Israel at Mount Sinai was given in written form in the model of contemporary treaties. Several references—Exod. 17:14; 24:4–8; 34:27; Num. 33:1f.—

undeniably credit Moses with writing. When the content of Exodus–Deuteronomy is taken at face value it is apparent that Moses was personally associated with most of the content as leader of Israel and mediator between them and God. It seems reasonable that Moses committed to writing the collection of laws, the details concerning the tabernacle, the instructions concerning various offerings, the installation of the priesthood, the instructions concerning the importance and significance of the feasts and seasons they were to observe, and combined this with an account of the events that occurred under his leadership. All of this was essential for coming generations of Israelites to realize that God had chosen them, manifested His love and mercy toward them in delivering them from Egyptian bondage, and had made known to them through Moses the covenant way of life so that through their personal devotion and commitment they would express their love for God, thereby fulfilling the law. The primacy of writing down important material in contemporary culture certainly is applicable when the revelation of God to Israel at Mount Sinai is recognized.

If there ever was a historic situation where a written document would have been considered important in the ancient Near East, it was the occasion in which Moses gave his farewell to the Israelites on the Moab plains before his death. He focused attention upon the unique divine revelation at Mount Sinai in which a special relationship between them and God was established. His basic concern was that this unique relationship with God should be maintained in a wholehearted exclusive devotion to and love for God not only by them but also by coming generations. To preserve it for posterity, Moses provided the law in written copies to be kept by the ark, according to Deuteronomy 31. The priests were charged with the responsibility to teach the people and provide copies for future leaders of Israel. Oral dissemination to every household was made through the public reading of the law every seven years. It would indeed have been inappropriate in the light of contemporary practice if Moses had left the content of God's great revelation to Israel to the process of oral transmission to posterity without taking advantage of preserving this in written form.

Based on the witness of contemporary culture and the internal claims of the Pentateuch itself, the present writer regards the first five books as essentially the work of Moses in interpreting the Old Testament, giving emphasis to the basic idea of the God-man relationship. Crucially significant is the Sinaitic revelation in which God spoke to Israel through Moses. Out of this issued the written word of divine revelation marking the birth of the Old Testament canon. With this in written form, the background for the God-man relationship is given in Genesis, which is unparalleled in literature and history as an introduction. With Moses as the great prophet, a written record is provided which was authoritative for Joshua and his generation of Israelites as well as posterity. By God-fearing people the Pentateuch was regarded as God's revelation and was supplemented by the prophets throughout Old Testament times.

BIBLIOGRAPHY FOR THE DOCUMENTARY-
HYPOTHESIS INTERPRETATION OF THE
PENTATEUCH

Layman's Guides

Bible Guides. W. Barclay and F. F. Bruce, eds. Nashville, Tenn.: Abingdon Press.

Layman's Bible Commentaries. B. H. Kelly, ed. Toronto: Ryerson Press.

Torch Bible Commentaries. John Marsh and Alan Richardson, eds. London: Christian Movement Press. New York: Macmillan.

Westminster Guides to the Bible. Edwin M. Good, ed. Philadelphia: Westminster Press.

Notes and study helps in *The Oxford Annotated Bible.* New York: Oxford University Press.

Textbooks

Anderson, B. W. *Understanding the Old Testament.* Englewood Cliffs, N.J.: Prentice-Hall, 1957.

Beebe, H. Keith. *The Old Testament.* Belmont, Calif.: Dickenson Publishing Co., 1970.

Gottwald, Norman. *A Light to the Nations.* New York: Harper & Row, 1959.

Larue, Gerald R. *Old Testament Life and Literature.* Boston: Allyn and Bacon, 1968.

Williams, Jay G. *Understanding the Old Testament.* New York: Barron's Educational Series, 1972.

BIBLIOGRAPHY FOR THE MOSAIC-AUTHORSHIP INTERPRETATION OF THE PENTATEUCH

Archer, Gleason. *A Survey of Old Testament Introduction.* Chicago: Moody Press, 1964.

Harrison, R. K. *Introduction to the Old Testament.* Grand Rapids, Mich.: Eerdmans, 1969.

Kitchen, Kenneth A. *Ancient Orient and Old Testament.* Chicago: Inter-Varsity Press, 1966.

Kline, Meredith G. *Treaty of the Great King.* Grand Rapids, Mich.: Eerdmans, 1963.

————. *The Structure of Biblical Authority.* Grand Rapids, Mich.: Eerdmans, 1972.

Schultz, Samuel J. *The Old Testament Speaks.* New York: Harper & Row, 2nd ed., 1970.

————. *The Prophets Speak.* New York: Harper & Row, 1968.

————. *Deuteronomy—Gospel of Love.* Chicago: Moody Press, 1971.

Young, E. J. *An Introduction to the Old Testament.* Grand Rapids, Mich.: Eerdmans, 1949.

VI

GOD'S PEOPLE IN
THE LAND OF PROMISE

The Israelites were God's people delivered out of Egypt and divinely chosen to occupy the land of Canaan. Through the covenant treaty at Mount Sinai they had entered into a vital and unique relationship with God. How this particular identity with God affected their total pattern of action and behavior in the post-Mosaic period is in part recorded in the books of Joshua, Judges, and Ruth.

THE BOOK OF THE LAW

In the treaty renewal covenant according to Deuteronomy, Moses outlined the basic principles which were to govern their pattern of living as they crossed the river Jordan and occupied the land of Canaan. In chapters 5 to 11 he delineated their responsibilities in maintaining a wholehearted exclusive devotion and love Godward, warning them against the dangers of the sordid polytheism existing among the Canaanites. In the following chapters Moses expounded the law of love as applied to the Israelites in their relationship with one another in matters of civic and religious responsibilities. In interpreting the core of God's revelation to them, Moses did not emphasize legalism or a legalistic system but stressed the basic importance of love for God in their responsibility in turn to reflect God's love for them to their fellow men in daily relationship with one another.

Joshua was the divinely designated leader in the continuance of this relationship between God and His people. He was not the recipient of extensive revelation as had been given through Moses. Joshua was commissioned as leader to direct the Israelites in living as God's holy people guided by the theological principles set forth by Moses. Consequently the attitude of Joshua toward the "book of the law" provided through Moses was clearly indicated. This was authoritative for him and his people (Josh. 1). There is no suggestion or inference that the Israelites decided to adopt the law of Moses by popular vote. It was their canon and was authoritative for them because they were God's people. Their relationship with God—established at Sinai and confirmed in a renewal treaty under Moses—was the determining factor in recognizing this collection of laws as governing their total pattern of living.

What right did the Israelites have to enter the land of Canaan, kill the inhabitants, and occupy the land as their own possession? What justification was there for them to shed blood against the background of the Sinaitic revelation in which they were commanded not to kill? Did the Israelites under Joshua reflect a sub-Christian culture in which war was tolerated?

In considering these questions the dating of Deuteronomy, Joshua, and Judges emerges as a significant factor in biblical interpretation. From the standpoint of a post-Davidic dating for these books they reflect the theological perspective of creative authors who combined the oral and written traditions of Israel's past. When these books are taken seriously as unfolding the behavioral pattern of the Israelites as God's covenant people, then the interpretation of these events finds its theological basis in Deuteronomy as the canonical foundation. The question of Israel's right to exterminate the Canaanites and occupy their land takes on a perspective that is God–Israel oriented.

EXTERMINATION OF THE CANAANITES

The instructions of Moses were explicit and clear: the Israelites were divinely commanded to kill the Canaanites and occupy their land (Deut. 7:16–26). The Canaanites were idolatrous and were committed to a pattern of living that could not be tolerated by a people wholly devoted to God. What Moses pointed out in warnings about the inhabitants of Canaan has been confirmed by archaeological findings in modern times.

Polytheism dominated and permeated the religion of the Canaanites. Their many gods, with Baal as chief, were worshiped as the providers of rainfall and fertility, crops and successful adventures in business. Attached to their centers of worship, usually on high places, were male and female prostitutes who made fertility rites available. The fertility of land, herds, flocks, and people was magically assured through sacred prostitution. Women would treasure the possession of mother goddess figurines assuming that this would assure them of pregnancy. It was considered proper to sacrifice the first-born son to curry favor, or to bury a child in a pottery bowl in the foundation of a new house in the hope that this would prosper the owner and his family.

Since the gods of the Canaanites had no moral character, it is not surprising that the morality of the people was extremely low. The brutality and immorality in the stories about these gods is far worse than anything else found in the Near East. Since this was reflected in the Canaanite society, the Canaanites in Joshua's day practiced child sacrifice, sacred prostitution, and snake worship—all of which were forbidden to the Israelites— in their rites and ceremonies associated with religion. Naturally their civilization had gained a momentum of degeneration and had the potential of being a demoralizing influence upon the Israelites (Deut. 18:9–14).

The Israelites were commissioned to execute judgment upon

these wicked inhabitants. They were acting as God's agents in bringing punishment upon the sinful generation of Canaanites living at the time of Joshua (Deut. 7:1–6).

Is the God of the Old Testament a God of war, judgment, and wrath, and the God whom Jesus revealed the Father of mercy and the God of love? Did the revelation through Moses portray a God of law and judgment which was replaced by a God of mercy and love through the teaching of Jesus and Paul?

In the heart of the Sinaitic revelation the basic attitude of God toward man is explicitly stated: punishment for those who hate God and lovingkindness for those who love God (Exod. 20:5–6). This principle can be traced through the Scriptures as God's relationship with man is delineated. God is merciful and just, executing judgment, but it is significant to note that mercy precedes judgment in His relationship with man. For the purpose of considering God's judgment upon the Canaanites, brief consideration will be given to God's relationship with mankind throughout biblical times in matters of mercy and judgment.

MERCY PRECEDES JUDGMENT

Man's beginning was cradled in the mercy and love of the Lord God (Gen. 2–3). Given dominion over all creatures, man was entrusted with the garden of Eden. When man sinned through disobedience, mercy preceded judgment in that God assured victory through the seed of the woman so that Adam and Eve had a hope to sustain them as they were subjected to the consequences of the curse. When the sinfulness of the human race precipitated divine judgment (Gen. 6:1–8), a 120-year period of mercy preceded the flood which destroyed all of the human race with the exception of Noah and his family.

In the days of Abraham, God's judgment came upon the population centers of Sodom and Gomorrah "because their sin is very grave" (Gen. 18–19). The period of Lot's residence among these people provided an extension of God's mercy through the life of righteous Lot. Although all the inhabitants of Sodom and Gomorrah were warned of impending doom, no one took Lot seriously so that only his family escaped with him. Here again God would have shown mercy if ten righteous people had been found in these wicked cities.

Judgment upon the Egyptians was preceded by a period of mercy during which the king of Egypt was given the opportunity to comply with God's request. In response to the demonstration of God's power through the period of the plagues the Israelites believed in God, but the Egyptians resisted as Pharaoh hardened his heart.

Even the Israelites precipitated divine judgment in a crisis at Kadesh. Everyone above the age of twenty excepting Caleb and Joshua was subjected to death in the wilderness and denied participation in the fulfillment of the promise to the nation to occupy the land of Canaan. Having witnessed the mighty acts of God displayed in their deliverance from the powerful Egyptians, they had a reasonable basis to believe with Joshua and Caleb that God would also aid them in overcoming the formidable occupants of Canaan. Since they had left Egypt, God's mercy had been manifested to them in daily care as manna and water were supplied to them miraculously en route through the wilderness. For nearly four decades the nation of Israel was delayed in the barren desert while the older generation faced the reality of God's judgment upon them because they "have grumbled against Me." With this verdict came the divine promise to the younger generation that "they shall know the land which you have rejected" (Num. 14:26–31).

Did mercy precede judgment as far as the Canaanites were concerned? Had they been exposed to any opportunity to know about God?

Even in the days of the ancient patriarchs the Canaanites had been exposed to the true God. When Abraham, Isaac, and Jacob lived in Canaan they worshiped God. A mark of Abraham wherever he lived was that he built an altar unto God. This could not be hidden and gave public witness that he had a vital relationship with the creator of heaven and earth. Melchizedek, who was king of Salem and priest of the Most High God, also was known for his devotion to God. In the days of Abraham the iniquity of the Canaan inhabitants was great but the Amorites were not yet "ripe for punishment" (Gen. 15:16). Centuries of divine mercy were extended to them while the Israelites lived in Egypt.

When the Israelites left Egypt, the news penetrated Canaan that "the Lord your God is God in heaven above and on the earth below" (Josh. 2:11). In the destruction of Jericho provision was made for the safety of Rahab and all who took refuge in her house.

The Gibeonites not only heard about all the mighty acts of God in behalf of Israel en route from Egypt to Canaan as well as the conquest of Jericho and Ai, but they had knowledge of the divine command through Moses that divine judgment was about to come upon them through conquest (Josh. 9:24). They were doomed to extermination. Consequently, they used deceptive means to save their lives—very likely the best they knew as far as the resources of their culture were concerned. The facts emerge in the record that not only Gibeon but also the cities of Chephirah, Beeroth, and Kiriath-jearim were spared destruction in the conquest of Canaan. Subsequently the Gibeonites had the opportunity of serving the Israelites and were privileged to participate in the total pattern of Israelite life in serving and worshiping God as provided in Deuteronomy.

The divine judgment upon the Canaanite inhabitants was punitive. Whereas the time for the termination of the godless culture of Sodom and Gomorrah had come in patriarchal times, the cup of iniquity of the Amorites was filled to the limit when Joshua was commanded to occupy the land of Canaan. For centuries divine judgment was postponed as God's mercy was extended to them. Special warning came to them as they heard of Israel's God bringing them out of Egypt and an additional four decades of mercy were extended while Israel was delayed in the desert wanderings.

God's judgment upon the Canaanites was also preventative. If they were permitted to continue in this godless pattern of living they would entice the Israelites to break their relationship with God by worshiping the gods of the Canaanites. Through fraternization and intermarriage the Israelites themselves would precipitate God's judgment upon themselves by conforming to the godless culture of their environment.

From the long-range perspective of God's eternal relationship with man, it was an act of mercy to terminate a culture that was becoming more sinful with each passing generation. If infants are the recipients of God's everlasting mercy it was providential to exterminate a civilization that was increasingly guilty of perpetuating snake worship, sacred prostitution, and child sacrifice in their religious rites and ceremonies. Divine judgment prevented future generations from incurring the same condemnation.

Centuries later God did show mercy to the large population center of Nineveh. When the Ninevites were confronted with their sinfulness through the preaching of the prophet Jonah, they turned to God in repentance. That generation experienced divine favor and the destruction of that great Assyrian capital was postponed for more than a century.

The severest judgment upon the Israelites in Old Testament times came in the destruction of Jerusalem in 586 B.C. This catastrophic event—the burning of the temple, the razing of Jerusalem, and the termination of the Davidic rule in Canaan —was preceded by four decades of warning by the prophet Jeremiah. As the religious and political Israelite culture permeated by materialism disintegrated, Jeremiah warned that they should not trust in their wisdom, riches, or power, but that it was important for them to realize that God shows unfailing love, justice, and righteousness in all His relationships with mankind (Jer. 9:23–24). Living through this terrible experience of seeing God's judgment executed upon Jerusalem, Jeremiah concludes that "the Lord's true love is surely not spent, nor has his compassion failed" (Lam. 3:22).

The apostle Paul undoubtedly had a better understanding of the records of Joshua concerning the extermination of the Canaanites than the twentieth-century reader. His knowledge of God most assuredly must have been based upon the Old Testament, which constituted the Scriptures for him as he studied them at Jerusalem. To him God of the Old Testament was the "father of mercies" (Cor. 1:3). Repeatedly Paul, in his preaching and his writings, warns that ultimately everyone must stand in judgment before God and that this age will bring about the consummation in which all non-God-fearing people will be subjected to the wrath of God and that the God-fearing people will continue to enjoy God's mercy forever.

The divine judgment upon the Canaanites is in accord with the basic revelation at Mount Sinai that God exercises judgment upon those who hate Him and mercy toward those who fear Him. God's judgment—executed upon the Canaanites through Joshua—will ultimately be divinely projected upon all sinful humanity. This is consistent with the teaching of Jesus who plainly taught that the wrath of God is upon all men except those who respond by faith to God's love manifested through Jesus Christ and thus are spared eternal condemnation. It is consistent with the teaching of Jeremiah and the other Old Testament prophets as well as with Paul and the apostles who proclaimed God's message after the fullness of the revelation that came through Jesus.

CONFIRMATION OF ISRAEL'S RELATIONSHIP WITH GOD

As Israel entered Canaan the mighty acts of God were manifested to make them as well as their enemies conscious of God's identification with His people. For the new generation this was vitally significant.

Forty years had passed since the older generation that died in the wilderness had experienced the crossing of the Red Sea that miraculously separated them from the Egyptians. In the crossing of the Jordan, a similar miracle occurred bringing this new generation into the land promised to Abraham and his descendants. Twelve stones were erected as a memorial to remind coming generations of God's provision in these two significant events:

> so that all the nations of the earth will realize that Jehovah is the
> mighty God, and
> so that all of you will worship Him forever (4:24).

Neither the Passover nor circumcision had been observed while the Israelites were under divine judgment wandering in the wilderness. Circumcision had been the sign of the God-man relationship beginning with Abraham. For the generation that had refused to trust God circumcision had lost its significance, since they were not realizing the fulfillment of the divine promise to enter Canaan. For the new generation under Joshua the rite of circumcision physically identified them as God's people. The years of desert wandering may have given the Egyptians cause to taunt the Israelites with abandonment by God, but the renewal of the Red Sea miracle at Jordan provided public testimony to the fact that God was with them. Obedience in the administration of circumcision brought them into a renewed consciousness of their covenant relationship with God going back to the time of Abraham.

Now the Israelites were in a standing before God so that they could observe the Passover with understanding and appreciation, since no uncircumcised person was allowed to eat the Passover. As God's people in the land of promise they were privileged to enjoy the fruit of the land and had no more need of a daily supply of manna.

CONQUEST OF CANAAN

The conquest of Jericho was primarily a religious rather than a military experience. In preparation for this sample victory, Joshua had a divine encounter in which God revealed Himself in human form and identified Himself as "captain of the host of the Lord" (Josh. 5:3–15). Like Moses at the burning bush, Joshua removed his sandals, realizing that he was on holy ground. As the Israelites marched around Jericho, the ark in the midst of the armed men realistically made them conscious of God's presence among them. Since God was executing judgment a ban was placed upon all of Jericho—property, livestock, and people —excepting Rahab and the people taking refuge with her and the treasures that were subsequently deposited in the tabernacle. Achan through his disobedience not only precipitated judgment upon himself and probably his family but also upon the nation in the defeat of Ai (cf. Josh. 7 and 22:20). Subsequently Ai was conquered.

After the conquest of Jericho and Ai which opened a wedge in central Canaan, Joshua assembled Israel for a renewal of the covenant at Shechem. God's presence with Joshua had been attested through the duplication of miracles in the crossing of the Jordan and victory over hostile forces similar to those Moses experienced during his leadership of Israel. Moses had given specific instructions (Deut. 27) that the Israelites should assemble in the natural amphitheater flanked by the slopes of the mountains of Ebal and Gerizim for the public reading of the law, to build an altar for worshiping God, and to inscribe the law of Moses on stone for the public to read. Inscribed stelae of this kind have been found in the Near East—the code of Hammurabi, the Merneptah stele, and others. The rockface inscription at Behistun in Media of a later period was about three times as long as the book of Deuteronomy. The observance of this religious ceremony of treaty renewal—probably held at Shechem which is located between these two mountains—provided the cultic confirmation of Joshua as the true successor to Moses as the leader of Israel.

Comparatively brief is the account concerning the conquest of Canaan southward and northward. Having made a treaty with the Gibeonites the Israelites were drawn into a battle with the Amorite kings constituting the southern confederacy. Through divine aid Joshua experienced a smashing victory and gained control of Canaan down to Kadesh-barnea and Gaza. The resistance of the Canaanites was broken in the battle near the waters of Merom and the destruction of the city of Hazor. Subsequently, Joshua allotted the conquered territory to the tribes for their occupation, giving forty-eight cities throughout the land to the Levites.

The blueprint for life in Canaan had been delineated by Moses in Deuteronomy and preceding books. The leaders of Israel—the Levites, elders, judges, and other officers—were to guide the people in executing justice in their daily relationships with one another according to the law of Moses. The Levites had special responsibility to teach the law and to guide the people in expressing their exclusive devotion to God in their total pattern of living as God's holy people.

Before Joshua died he publicly expressed his concern about the unique relationship existing between the Israelites and God. Summoning the Israelites in a general assembly to Shechem, Joshua addressed them informally as indicated in chapter 23 and then led them in a public renewal of the covenant which follows the model of ancient suzerainty treaties in contemporary cultures.

As Moses had renewed the Sinaitic treaty before his death, so Joshua publicly in dialogue form led Israel in renewing their covenant relationship with God in his final appeal. In the preamble he identified "the Lord, the God of Israel" as the author of the covenant. In the historical prologue (24:2b–13) Joshua reminded them of the fact that their ancestors had been idolators but beginning with Abraham God had cared for them from generation to generation and that God had graciously cared for them so that now they were actually living in the land of Canaan. The stipulation of this covenant is simply expressed in the reminder, "fear the Lord and serve him in sincerity and truth."

Exclusive loyalty and wholehearted devotion are basic. No idolatry can be tolerated. Realizing that each individual must make his own choice, Joshua expressed his personal decision: "as for me and my family we will serve the Lord." Warning them that a curse awaited them if they turned to idols (24:20), Joshua called them to be witnesses of their affirmation in this renewal treaty (24:22). Provision was made for the perpetuation of the covenant for coming generations in the terms written "in the book of the law of God." Very likely what Joshua provided in writing was deposited by the ark with the copies of the law that had been written by Moses (Deut. 21:26).

VII

THE KINGDOM
ESTABLISHED

The promise of the land of Canaan—divinely delineated from the initial revelation to Abraham and enlarged through Moses —was realized under Joshua. As long as Moses was with the Israelites they received continual communication concerning God's guidance. Joshua as divinely appointed successor led the Israelites in the conquest and possession of the land promised to them as their inheritance.

PROVISIONS BY MOSES

Provisions for implementing the pattern of living as God's chosen people in Canaan had already been revealed through Moses. He outlined for them the basic structure of organization as to priestly responsibilities under Aaron and the Levites. Prophets were anticipated in a future ministry to remind coming generations of the Words of God given through Moses and to supplement God's message in application to contemporary conditions.

Even during their Egyptian captivity, the Israelites had a representative group of men known as elders (Exod. 3:16). Moses collaborated with these men in preparation for his encounter with Pharaoh. Later Moses was surrounded by seventy elders (Exod. 34:1) who shared some of the civic responsibilities with him. In anticipation of Israel's occupation of Canaan, Moses indicated that these elders should also serve as judges in apprehending murderers (Deut. 19:12), in conducting inquests (Deut. 21:2), and in settling matrimonial disputes (Deut. 22:15; 25:7). The transition from Israel's organization and encampment under Moses to a settled state in Palestine brought normal and expected changes in administration. Cities throughout the land had officials who probably came under the general classification of elders or who had responsibilities with them. Some of these are mentioned as heads of tribes (Deut. 5:23; 29:10) and as officers and judges (Josh. 8:33). Details about the number of elders for *each* city are not given. The city of Succoth had seventy-seven (Judg. 8:14). In later history a national body of elders is referred to in various periods (cf. I Sam. 8:4; II Sam. 5:3; I Kings 8:1, 3; 20:7; 21:8; II Kings 10:2; 21:2; 23:1; Ezek. 8:1; 14:1; 20:1).

The Levites were given responsibility for religious functions and the maintaining of worship. By virtue of sparing every first-born son in the Passover experience, God expected the oldest son in each family to be dedicated to Him. Subsequently the Levites were designated as official substitutes for the first-born in each family (Num. 1–4) and the tithe was designated for their support (Num. 18:21–24).

With the erection of the tabernacle, the Levites were given the immediate responsibility of caring for the central sanctuary. The Levites in turn were under the direct supervision of Aaron and his sons (Num. 8:19). Aaron was the spiritual leader of Israel in matters of worship and continual ministration at the tabernacle. Under Moses he was inducted into this office (Lev. 8; Exod. 39) so that Aaron and his sons had the priestly duties of officiating at the tabernacle.

In the transition from Israel's pattern of living under Moses' leadership to that of settlement in Canaan the duties of Levites, including the priests, were somewhat adjusted and modified as supervision was decentralized. The Levites were assigned to live in forty-eight cities set aside for their use throughout Palestine (Num. 35:1ff.; Josh. 21:1ff.). In outlining the anticipated responsibilities it is quite likely that some of the duties assigned to the priests were delegated to the Levites at large. While the tabernacle with its attending priests was geographically limited to one place, the ministry of the Levites was made available throughout the land.

Additional duties assigned to the Levites involving them in various social, civic, and religious ministries were, as given in Deuteronomy: (1) to serve as judges in cases involving difficult decisions (17:8–9); (2) to regulate the supervision of lepers (24:8); (3) to guard the copies of the book of the law (17:18); and (4) to assist Moses in the covenant-renewal ceremony (27:9). Some of these responsibilities pertained to various Levitical cities, while others were limited to the central sanctuary.

Through the prophetic ministry the Israelites were to maintain a continual consciousness of God's will for them. In addition to that which had been revealed through Moses and provided for them in written form, there was the need of knowing God's will as it pertained to the current developments in each generation. Through the Urim and Thummim, which were kept in the high priest's breastplate (Exod. 28:30; Lev. 8:8), the priest was endowed with the ability to declare the will of God. Significantly, this provision is made with the ordination of Joshua to leadership (Num. 27:18–23). Whereas this seemed to be the means of providing a knowledge of God's will to those who inquired, the ministry of a prophet as outlined by Moses was that of positive and active proclamation of His will. In two passages Moses assures the Israelites that men will come as God's representatives to make known His messages as needed. In the course of Israel's history, the ministry of men who were especially commissioned to speak God's messages apparently replaced the use of the Urim and Thummim by the priests.

The priests were the custodians of the law. To them was

committed the written copy of the agreement between God and His people Israel. It was their responsibility to make the content of this written copy available to the people as well as the leaders throughout subsequent generations.

Parents were under obligation to teach their children about their relationship with God. The home was the basic institution in which the Israelites were to maintain this vital relationship with God and contagiously impart it to each succeeding generation. In the home the growing children were continually made conscious of God by numerous external means as outlined in Deuteronomy 4–6. Parents were admonished to remind the next generation of God's mighty acts in redeeming them out of Egypt. This great miracle of redemption they should never forget as a nation. The core and essence of parental teaching was not merely an intellectual knowledge and understanding of the law or primarily orthodox doctrine but was, rather, a proper conception of knowledge and reverence for God. The "fear of God" so frequently referred to throughout the Bible is not a matter of "being afraid of God" but a practical understanding that the God who had redeemed Israel was a God of love and that His mercy would be extended everlastingly to those who loved and revered Him. This concept of God could be effectively taught to children only by precept and example. As parents expressed this wholehearted commitment and love toward God in their daily lives, the children became acquainted with a pattern of living in which God was continually and consistently recognized. The septennial public reading of the covenant requirements aided in the oral dissemination of the law to the entire nation.

The leaders of Israel were also expected to conform to the law of Moses. Their responsibility was to set an example of faithfully observing the requirements revealed through Moses and preserved in written form. Whether the leader was a military general, a judge, a priest, a prophet, or a king, it was his first duty to acknowledge the fact that he was a member of God's covenant nation. He was expected to exemplify a wholehearted commitment to God. Although copies of the law may have been rare and expensive at that time, Moses made provision so that a ruler in Israel was to be provided by the priests with a personal copy. Kingship in Israel was unique in that the king did not have sole authority, but like his people was to be obedient to the law.

The prophetic function of reminding the Israelites in post-Mosaic times of the mutual responsibilities between God and Israel was exemplified in subsequent history. Leaders vary in their particular responsibility depending upon the circumstances and needs in their generation. In the course of Israel's transition from a theocracy to a kingship this prophetic function becomes more essential.

WHEN JUDGES RULED

The moral and spiritual breakdown came in the post-Joshua era. The newer generations, not having witnessed the mighty acts of God which had been manifested through Joshua, turned to idolatry. This apostasy was a breaking of the first commandment and indicated an obvious neglect of that wholehearted love and commitment that was so essential in their relationship with God. So prevalent was the apostasy that God's judgment was exercised through invading nations. These oppressions were designed to make the Israelites conscious of their apostasy (Judg. 2:20–23). Intermarriage with those who were not devoted to God resulted in disintegration of the home. Instead of being taught by their parents to revere and love God, the children were led astray into idolatry. The severity of these oppressions repeatedly stimulated repentance and ultimately brought relief as God responded to their appeals for mercy.

God's communication to the Israelites during the era of the judges came through mighty acts as well as through the prophetic word. Relatively little detail is given in the biblical account, but the basic fact throughout is that these military leaders were motivated to action by divine initiative. Concerning some of these men it is recorded that the spirit of the Lord came upon them (Judg. 3:10;11:20; 13:25). For others such as Gideon and Samson extensive details are given concerning their preparation for delivering the Israelites from their oppressors. Although they had the law of Moses they did not obey it. Perhaps the question raised by Gideon was repeatedly asked in succeeding generations, "where are all the miracles our fathers tell us of . . .?" (Judg. 6:13.) By raising up these judges God made Himself known to successive generations as they witnessed and experienced deliverance through miracles.

Divine communication came also through theophanies. Angelic messengers appeared in connection with Gideon's call and Samson's birth. Through these God made known His will regarding the particular situation in response to Israel's cry for divine aid. Messages of prediction with the assurance of divine deliverance from oppressing nations were given in both instances (Judg. 6:14; 13:5).

The words "prophet" and "prophetess" appear once each in the book of Judges. Little is known about Deborah beyond the fact that she was recognized by the Israelites for an effective ministry in rendering judgment. She spoke as God's messenger to Barak, indicating that through him divine deliverance from Canaanite oppression was in the offing. The predictive element in her message was the promise that the superior forces of Sisera would be defeated (Judg. 4:7, 14). This organic prediction was fulfilled in divinely timed weather conditions that gave Barak the advantage over the Canaanites (Judg. 5:4, 20). The secondary prediction involving the death of Sisera by Jael, instead of by soldiers on the field of battle, made it apparent that God was in control and aided His people.

An unnamed prophet is briefly noted in the days of Gideon (Judg. 6:7–10). He came as God's messenger during the Midianite oppression when the Israelites were appealing for divine aid. His message was brief and to the point. They had not obeyed God who had delivered them out of Egypt and enabled them to occupy Canaan but had turned to idols. Instead of revering God they had revered idols.

How extensively the priests and elders disseminated the knowledge of the written law during the era of the judges is not indicated. It is apparent, however, that Jephthah as well as the parents of Samson reflect rather detailed acquaintance with Israel's history and their sacrifices as recorded in the Pentateuch (Judg. 11; 13). The only reference to the central sanctuary is in Judg 18:1, indicating that the tabernacle was located at Shiloh. The last five chapters in Judges do reflect the religious and moral laxity prevalent throughout the nation when every man did as he pleased.

The low ebb of Israel's religion is realistically portrayed in the life of Eli, who had the responsibility of serving as both judge and priest at Shiloh. Eli's failure to teach his sons, Hophni and Phinehas, the essence of Israel's religion was apparent in their lack of respect and love for God and for their fellow Israelites. Serving as priests they had no respect for God (I Sam. 2:12). Instead of exemplifying reverence for God and teaching the requirements as projected in the Mosaic revelation, these sons took advantage of the Israelites who brought their sacrifices to the tabernacle in Shiloh. In addition Hophni and Phinehas were guilty of immoral behavior with the women who assembled at the tabernacle (I Sam. 2:12–17, 22–25).

Israel's religion declined to such a naturalistic conception of God that the Israelites prevailed upon the sons of Eli to bring the ark of the covenant, which symbolized God's presence, into the battlefield (I Sam. 4:1–22). Theologically the people were correct in that God was more powerful than the enemy and would not let Himself be captured, but they were mistaken in their belief that the presence of the ark would bring them victory. Their jubilant reaction to the presence of the ark in the battlefield was soon silenced in utter defeat. When the news came that his sons had been killed and the ark of God had been taken by the Philistines, Eli, still sensitive to the seriousness of the situation, died of shock.

God was not limited to the establishment. In all likelihood the city of Shiloh was destroyed by Philistines. At least the ark was not returned to Shiloh when it was released by the enemy. Centuries later Jeremiah (7:14) pointed to the ruins of Shiloh and warned his generation that Jerusalem with its temple would likewise be destroyed. Neither was God limited to the established priesthood of Eli and his family. Lacking a vital relationship with God they were judged and replaced.

With apostasy prevailing at Shiloh, God revealed himself through God-fearing laity. Hannah expressed her concern through prayer and subsequently became the mother of a son through whom the consciousness of God was restored to Israel. Concurrently, during this period when Samuel was born and reared in the tabernacle environment, an unnamed man of God came to deliver a message of judgment to Eli. Speaking for God, he warned Eli that he had failed to honor God in his lack of disciplining his sons. This prophet predicted judgment in the death of Eli's sons and the ultimate removal of his family from the priesthood in Israel (I Sam. 2:27–36). The reminder by this man of God that Eli's family had been chosen to serve when Israel was delivered from Egypt reflects a knowledge of the Pentateuchal laws and narratives. Although the organic prediction of the removal of Eli's family from the priesthood did not occur for several generations, the incidental prophecy about the death of Eli's sons was fulfilled in his lifetime.

God's revelation was further enlarged through Samuel in both positive and negative aspects. Samuel's call to be a prophet provided constructive leadership, while the impending judgment upon the house of Eli was reaffirmed. Samuel's first message was a solemn word of rebuke and judgment for the national leader of Israel who had failed in his parental and priestly responsibilities. Eli's iniquity was beyond purging by sacrifice or offering (I Sam. 3:11–14).

With Eli's death, Samuel emerged as the national leader of

Israel. His primary concern was for the Israelites to renew their spiritual relationship with God. He reminded them of the vital truth that they had broken the first commandment in turning to idolatry (I Sam. 7:3). He predicted that God would give them victory over the Philistines if they would turn to Him in repentance. After Samuel officiated in sacrifice and prayed for his people, God's revelation to Israel was manifested in His mighty acts on their behalf. The Philistines were defeated through divine intervention (I Sam. 7:10). By emphasizing the importance of Israel's relationship with God as outlined in the written body of revelation that had been given through Moses, the prophet Samuel led Israel back into a pattern of living in which they enjoyed God's favor and blessing.

Samuel was nationally recognized as a judge, a priest, and a prophet. Making his circuit annually throughout Israel, he served effectively as judge. In his priestly function he officiated at sacrifices at such cities as Ramah, Mizpah, Bethlehem, Gilgal, and other places. As a prophet he was known as the man of God (I Sam. 9:6–7, 10) and recognized throughout the land from Dan to Beersheba (I Sam. 3:19–21). When Samuel began to delegate his responsibilities, the Israelites requested a king. Consequently Samuel had a significant influence in Israel as they changed from theocracy to kingship.

Although Samuel advised the Israelites against having a king, it was divinely revealed to him that he should comply with their request. Subsequently he anointed Saul and later David as kings in Israel.

The uniqueness of Israel's relationship with God was to be maintained even in the transition to kingship. God's revelation to Samuel was explicit. Saul was anointed "prince over my people Israel" (I Sam. 9:16; 10:1). Consequently a king was under obligation to be obedient to God. As king he had stewardship responsibilities to rule over God's people with a fixed accountability to God. He, as well as the people, was subject to the law of God (Deut. 17:14–20).

Through Samuel the prophet, the conditions of success were outlined for Saul. Even though the Israelites belittled him, Saul was assured that the spirit of God would come upon him. Previously men like Gideon, Jephthah, and Samson had been endued for the purpose of giving Israel relief from oppressing enemies. Saul experienced a manifestation of God's spirit even before he was publicly anointed (I Sam. 10). Samuel in his role as prophet assured Saul and his people that if they would wholeheartedly love and serve God (I Sam. 12), they would be assured of His presence among them. Subsequently the spirit of God came upon Saul to effect a victory over the Ammonites. Later, when Saul disobeyed, warnings came repeatedly through Samuel. Yielding to impatience Saul acted foolishly in officiating at a sacrifice, which was a priestly duty (I Sam. 13). Instead of executing the assignment to punish the Amalekites, Saul substituted sacrifice for obedience and thus forfeited the kingdom.

Conditions worsened as Saul, in his attitude of defiance of the divinely revealed will of God as known to him through the Mosaic law and through Samuel, continued to rule. Concurrently God's message had come to Samuel that David had been chosen to be captain over God's inheritance, the people of Israel (I Sam. 13:14). When Samuel died, all the Israelites gathered to lament the death of this great prophet of the Lord (I Sam. 25:1).

THE DAVIDIC ERA

The life of David represents the epitome of God's revelation through one man who served as both prophet and king in Israel. In spite of his failures and shortcomings, David was genuinely and realistically concerned about his relationship with God. The Mosaic-theocratic rule in Israel found expression in David's reign and was never equaled after his death. Consequently the reign of David was repeatedly the point of reference in the prophetic messages as the ideal of the kingdom of Israel.

Throughout his life, David was sensitive in maintaining an attitude of dependence upon God and a wholehearted commitment to God as outlined in the Mosaic revelation. In his early years he learned to depend upon God for care and protection when he was responsible for his father's flocks (I Sam. 17:37). Concern for God's honor motivated David to trust Him to aid him in challenging Goliath (I Sam. 17:26). He was confident that through God's power manifested in this victory, the knowledge of God would be widely evident (I Sam. 17:46). Throughout the period when Saul sought his life, David was conscious of God's protection (Ps. 18, and others). Repeatedly he refused to kill the Lord's anointed (I Sam. 24:6).

When David was recognized as king of all Israel he demonstrated a genuine concern for public acknowledgment of God by making Jerusalem the center of worship. This ultimately led to plans to build a temple, but David himself was not permitted to execute this project. By organizing the priests and Levites, by purchasing a site for the temple, by making commercial arrangements with Hiram, the king of Tyre, and by writing numerous psalms for worship, David anticipated a national recognition and worship of God such as Israel had never before experienced as a powerful nation.

David was a brilliant militarist. Successfully he gained the military advantage over the surrounding nations and established the supremacy of Israel in the heart of the fertile crescent. These achievements were acknowledged by David as a manifestation of God's power. In Psalm 18 and II Samuel 22, he expresses his gratitude to God for His mighty acts in behalf of Israel. In this manner God's power was displayed in behalf of His covenant people through David, who was confirmed as captain of God's inheritance.

David maintained an attitude of compliance with the basic terms of Israel's covenant relationship with God as revealed through Moses. Idolatry, which was Israel's besetting sin during the era of the judges, is hardly mentioned in association with

David's reign as it is portrayed in the books of II Samuel and I Chronicles. At the close of his reign, David instructed Solomon to obey the law of Moses, calling to his attention the implications of obedience and disobedience (I Kings 2:3). With a similar emphasis, David charged the princes, the leaders, and the nation as a whole to give heed to God and His requirements (I Chron. 28:8). Love and devotion to God expressed in obedience was the key to Israel's enjoyment of God's continued blessing.

The prophetic revelation in Davidic times was supplemental to that which had been given previously. The prophets most active in association with David were Nathan and Gad. The former at first concurred with David in his plan to build the temple, but subsequent to God's revelation to him Nathan advised David to the contrary. The divine promise given through Nathan at this time assured David, however, that his throne would be established eternally (II Sam. 7). When David ignored God temporarily in taking Bathsheba as his wife at the expenditure of Uriah's life, it was Nathan the prophet who rebuked the king of Israel for his great sin.

The prophet Gad was another spokesman for God who ministered to King David in time of crisis. Apparently David was guilty of pride in the census that he conducted in spite of Joab's objections, and consequently judgment came upon Israel. Through Gad the divine message was made known to David and ultimately through this experience the site of the temple was purchased and fixed.

The vital relationship that David normally had with God is extensively and beautifully reflected in the psalms. Repeatedly he expresses his love and wholehearted devotion to God. Approximately seventy-five psalms are associated with David. In the penitential psalms, such as Psalm 32 and Psalm 51, David freely speaks of his deep sense of guilt and sinfulness as well as of his consciousness of God's abounding mercy in the personal forgiveness of his sin. In Psalms 21,37, and others, David as king of Israel expresses his confidence in God in whom is the source of blessing for his people. In Psalm 19 and similar passages he conveys his recognition of God's revelation in nature.

David's experience as expressed in Psalms 51 and 32 against the background of II Samuel 11–12 offers a realistic insight into personal religion in Old Testament times. Confession of sin was as essential to a vital relationship with God as it was later in New Testament times. When David prays "create in me a clean heart" he is as conscious of a supernatural work in his life as the New Testament writers are when they speak of "being born again," "a new creature in Christ," a "new life," and similar expressions. David's hope for forgiveness was not primarily vested in the sacrifices per se, but in the attitude expressed in a "broken and contrite heart" or a "broken spirit." The external or legalistic approach could never be a substitute for a vital personal relationship with God. Nor could offering and sacrifices serve in place of a contrite heart.

The divine guidance David identifies in Psalm 32:8 seems to have been as genuine in his life as that which is identified with the Holy Spirit in the fuller revelation in the New Testament.

In numerous psalms the messianic hopes are considerably enlarged through David, who had been assured through Nathan that his throne would be established forever. In Psalm 22 David portrays the suffering and death of the Messiah as well as the universal extension of God's kingdom. The hope of the resurrection is expressed in Psalm 16 and others. In the New Testament, Christ and the apostles acknowledge David as a prophet who spoke of future events such as the death and resurrection which were fulfilled in Jesus Christ, whom David in his psalms already had acknowledged as his Lord. The establishment of the universal kingdom as hopefully expressed by David was recognized in New Testament times as rightfully belonging to the future developments.

Through Solomon, God's revelation continued. He began his reign displaying the wisdom divinely imparted in response to his prayer, experienced the manifestation of God's presence as the divine glory filled the temple at the time of its dedication, and received the subsequent acclaim of surrounding nations. In the course of time, however, Solomon became lax in his relationship with God, ignored the Mosaic restrictions as given in Deuteronomy 17, and tolerated idolatry. Consequently, rival leaders rose to influence and power so that after Solomon's death the great Israelite kingdom was divided (I Kings 11). Though Solomon was acclaimed as the wisest man in history, he was usually ignored by the prophets, since he failed in maintaining a vital relationship with God.

In subsequent periods the kingdom of David is proclaimed as the ideal kingdom. Prophet after prophet used David and his kingdom as the point of reference when the hopes of restoration in the universal kingdom were outlined. The prevalence of the knowledge of God throughout David's kingdom marked a decided advance and realistic supplement to the Mosaic revelation. As king and prophet, David had a vivid perspective of the Messiah who would come as one of his descendants to establish a universal kingdom.

Date	Northern K.	Prophets	Southern K.	Assyria	Syria
931	*Jeroboam Dyn.* Jeroboam	Ahijah Shemaiah Iddo	Rehoboam Abijam		Rezon
909	Nadab *Baasha Dyn.* Baasha	Azariah Hanani Jehu	Asa		
885	Elah (Zimri) *Omri Dynasty* Omri (Tibni) Ahab	Elijah Micaiah Eliezer	Jehoshaphat	Ashurnarsipal	Benhadad
841	Ahaziah Joram *Jehu Dynasty* Jehu	Elisha Jehoiada Zechariah	Jehoram Ahaziah Athaliah Joash	Shalmaneser III	Hazael
	Jehoahaz Jehoash Jeroboam II	Jonah Hosea Amos	Amaziah Azariah		Benhadad
752	Zechariah *Last Kings* Shallum Menahem Pekahiah Pekah Hoshea	Isaiah Oded	Jotham Ahaz	Tiglath-pileser III Shalmaneser V Sargon II	Rezin
722	*Fall of Samaria*	Micah	Hezekiah Manasseh Amon	Sennacherib Esarhaddon Ashurbanipal	
640		Jeremiah Huldah (Ezekiel) (Daniel)	Josiah Jehoahaz Jehoiakim Jehoiachin Zedekiah	*Babylon* Nabopolassar Nebuchadnezzar	
586			*Fall of Jerusalem*		

VIII

GOD'S MESSAGE FOR
AN APOSTATE PEOPLE

The splendor of the greatness of the Davidic kingdom and the
glory of the temple glittering in gold as a dwelling place for God
in the midst of His chosen nation was no insurance against
apostasy. Because Solomon tolerated idolatrous shrines in the
environs of Jerusalem, the greatest kingdom Israel achieved in
Old Testament times was abruptly subjected to divine judgment in partition.

APOSTASY AND ITS CONSEQUENCES

The Davidic family continued to rule from Jerusalem over
the limited area known as Judah, or the Southern Kingdom, for
about three and a half centuries (931–586 B.C.). Less than ten
miles northward was the border of the Northern Kingdom,
identified frequently as Israel in the books of Kings and Chronicles or as Ephraim in the books of Hosea and Isaiah. This kingdom lasted only about two centuries (931–722 B.C.). Further to
the north and eastward the kingdom of Syria asserted its independence with Damascus as the capital capitulating to Assyria
in 732. Ten years later the Assyrians conquered Samaria and by
661 B.C. extended their conquest down into Egypt as far south
as Thebes.

Religiously these centuries in the history of God's chosen people are characterized by idolatry and apostasy. The Northern Kingdom as a whole had kings who ignored the Mosaic revelation proclaimed by the prophets and led the people into idolatrous ways. In the Southern Kingdom many kings on the Davidic throne defied the prophets but periodically great revivals occurred, notably under Jehoshaphat, Hezekiah, and Josiah.

Politically the balance of power shifted with the changing times. For nearly a half century warfare prevailed as the nations of Palestine struggled to establish their identity. With the rise of the third royal dynasty in 885, Omri promoted a policy of friendship with surrounding nations that made the Northern Kingdom so prosperous politically and economically that it continued to dominate Palestine for almost a half century under Ahab and his sons. About the time that Jehu led a revolution in 841 to overthrow the Omride rule, Hazael emerged as the powerful king of Syria and dominated Israel and Judah down to the turn of the century. Under Jeroboam II the Northern Kingdom attained an unprecedented peak of economic prosperity and political power that enabled them to dominate Judah as well as Syria. Following Jeroboam's death internal struggles for power weakened the Northern Kingdom so that Uzziah as king of Judah emerged as the powerful ruler who led a Palestinian coalition in which he temporarily stopped the Assyrian advance under Tiglath-pileser III in 742 B.C. Within five years after Uzziah's death Ahaz as king of Judah made a treaty with Assyria which precipitated the fall of Damascus and Samaria to the Assyrians. In the changing times that followed Assyria advanced its powerful influence down into Egypt with Judah often paying tribute as the price for survival. During the latter half of the seventh century, while the power of Assyria declined, the kingdom of Judah enjoyed about three decades of respite from foreign domination. With the fall of Nineveh in 612 B.C., the Assyrians capitulated to the Babylonians who subsequently conquered the Southern Kingdom, destroying Jerusalem with its temple in 586 B.C.

Throughout these centuries of stress and strain, prophet after prophet came to remind the people as well as the kings about that which had been revealed through Moses. Each prophet was vitally concerned with the man-God relationship. Idolatry, which seemed to be the besetting sin, provided external evidence that the people had departed from their wholehearted devotion and love for God. The social evils of the time reflected their lack of love for their fellow men. Prophet after prophet asserts that as long as inequity, injustice, and unrighteousness are evident in the oppression of the poor and the neglect of the widows and orphans, and preferential treatment is given to the privileged people in the courts, it is apparent that they do not love God wholeheartedly. Love for God is manifest in daily life as love for man is practiced.

GUIDANCE FOR NEW LEADERS

The prophet Ahijah explicitly exposed the reasons for the disintegration of the Davidic kingdom when he promised Jeroboam that he would be the ruler of the Northern Kingdom (I Kings 11:26–40). Solomon's failure to maintain a God-fearing attitude as David had done precipitated divine judgment. For David's sake the throne would be preserved on a limited basis. Jeroboam, however, was assured that his throne would be established on the condition of his obedience. Idolatry on his part would result in his forfeiting the kingdom.

Another prophet warned Jeroboam at the beginning of his reign about idolatry. This prophet is identified merely as a man of God from Judah (I Kings 13). Jeroboam disregarded the warnings about adhering to the law, erected altars, appointed priests to his liking, and set before Israel the example of idolatry. When the man of God rebuked Jeroboam for officiating at the altar in Bethel, the king ordered the arrest of the prophet. Two miracles were performed confirming his prophet as God's messenger. Jeroboam's arm was paralyzed and restored, and the altar was rent in accordance with the prophet's word. The latter should have provided undeniable evidence to the king as well as to his people that God was currently revealing Himself, making His will known through this prophet. In spite of this warning, Jeroboam persisted in his idolatrous ways, which precipitated God's judgment upon himself and his kingdom.

Shemaiah was the prophet in Judah at the crucial time when the Solomonic kingdom was partitioned. When Rehoboam planned to subdue the northern rebellion under Jeroboam by force, Shemaiah conveyed God's message warning the king not to interfere (I Kings 12:20–24). Rehoboam was sensitive to the prophet's message as he began his reign. His adherence to the law may have been stimulated by the Levites who were dismissed from priestly service by Jeroboam and in turn migrated in large numbers to the kingdom of Judah. When Rehoboam was established as king, he and his people became unfaithful in their devotion to God as prescribed in the law. Shemaiah once more had a message interpreting the current development, in which Shishak was threatening Jerusalem, as an act of God. In response to their repentance Rehoboam and the leaders were assured that Shishak's invasion would be limited and would not be final as far as Jerusalem was concerned (II Chron. 11–12).

REVERSING RELIGIOUS TRENDS

Azariah, the son of Oded, was empowered by the Spirit of God to bring a message of encouragement during an era when Asa took the initiative in a reform movement. Under Rehoboam and Abijah idol worship prevailed throughout the land of Judah, but Asa made extensive reforms in removing idolatry even to the point of demoting his mother, Maacah, from being queen (I Kings 15:11–13). Even though the priests converged en masse from all Palestine and took up residence in Judah in the days of Rehoboam and were used by King Abijah in his war against Jeroboam (II Chron. 13), the first two decades following Solomon's death were characterized by a dearth of teaching priests who were concerned about the law (II Chron. 15:3). When Asa, king of Judah, expressed a concern to seek after God and then experienced God's act of deliverance in victory over the Ethiopians, the prophet Azariah (Oded) encouraged Asa in his reformation. By the fifteenth year of his reign, Asa's revival in Judah drew not only the citizens of Judah but also those of the northern tribes to Jerusalem. This religious interest in participating in the revival in Jerusalem by the citizens of the Northern Kingdom led to the fortification of Ramah by King Baasha to prevent such pilgrimages.

The international crisis precipitated by this development provided the occasion for the prophet Hanani to deliver God's message of rebuke to Asa, king of Judah. Asa solved the problem of Baasha's aggression by using temple treasures to bribe Benhadad, king of Syria, into an alliance. When the latter attacked cities near Israel's northern border, Baasha abandoned the Ramah project, moving his armies north. Consequently Asa occupied Ramah to his own advantage. Hanani's criticism pertained to the man-God relationship which represented the core of the Mosaic covenant. Asa had lapsed in his wholehearted devotion to God and trusted in his own wisdom to solve this problem. He had experienced God's revelation in a mighty act of deliverance when he was faced by a superior force. Consequently he had experiential evidence for believing that God would have helped him in this crisis. Asa had acted foolishly by relying on his own wisdom. Reacting adversely to this rebuke the king imprisoned Hanani, causing the prophet to suffer for delivering God's message. Later during his reign, Asa himself was subjected to physical suffering, but even in this he did not return to an attitude of seeking after God. Hanani may be one of the prophets Hosea (8:9) refers to as being hated in the house of his God.

Jehu, the son of Hanani, was God's spokesman to announce judgment upon the dynasty of Baasha. Although he had been enabled to destroy the royal family of Jeroboam in judgment for their idolatrous ways, Baasha himself was guilty of idolatry. Divine judgment would come in a similar manner on the family of Baasha repeatedly throughout his reign (I Kings 16:1–8).

PROTESTING BAALISM

Elijah came with God's message during a period of unprecedented political power and national idolatry in the Northern Kingdom. Omri built Samaria as Israel's capital and successfully promoted a policy of friendship with surrounding nations so that his kingdom was stronger than it had been since its beginning in 931 under Jeroboam. The Israelite–Phoenician alliance was sealed by the marriage of Omri's son, Ahab, to Jezebel, the daughter of Ethbaal, king of Tyre. As a result idolatry was promoted to excess as Ahab and Jezebel made Baal worship the official religion of Israel. In Samaria a temple was erected to Baal. Even though Ahab provoked more divine displeasure than had any king before him (I Kings 16:30–33), God revealed Himself more extensively in miracles and specific guidance in Ahab's era through Elijah and Elisha than the Israelites had experienced since the time of Solomon.

Boldly Elijah faced Ahab when Jezebel was silencing the prophets of the Lord throughout the land (I Kings 18:4, 13). Elijah was concerned about the man-God relationship. The warning about the lack of rain conditioned Ahab and the people for the public assembly on Mount Carmel. Elijah's public prayer for a miraculous ignition of the sacrifice in order that the Israelites might know that the Lord God was the God of the patriarchs was answered (I Kings 18:36). Other predictions concerning the drought and subsequent rain were likewise fulfilled in accordance with Elijah's word. Consequently Elijah was established as a prophet in Israel by miracles even as Moses had been during the exodus.

Elijah had his times of discouragement. Threatened by Jezebel he fled southward where he experienced an angelic revelation at Beersheba, which strengthened him. At Mount Horeb in another divine revelation he received specific instructions to continue as God's servant (I Kings 19:9–18). When Elijah expressed concern about Israel's broken relationship with God, lamented the fact that the altars of God had been wrecked, and grieved over the martyred prophets, he was assured that there still were seven thousand God-fearing people who had not capitulated to idolatry. Elijah was encouraged by the predictions given relative to his continued service as a prophet, being made conscious anew of the fact that God controls the affairs of nations even as had been exemplified in Israel's history since Mosaic times. Included in his assignment were the replacements of the ruling families in both Israel and Syria. Elijah was also assured of the termination of the Baal-devoted dynasty which he was opposing. The prophetic ministry, on the other hand, would continue through his successor, Elisha. In this way Baalism would be countered by a threefold thrust in the rise of a strong aggressive king, Hazael, in Syria; in Jehu taking control in Israel; and in Elisha's supporting and continuing ministry. Almost immediately Elisha joined Elijah. Through the former both Hazael and Jehu were informed of their royal responsibilities.

Unnamed prophets were active during Ahab's reign. In I Kings 20 they were identified as "a prophet" in verse 20, as "a man of God" in verse 28, and as "a certain man of the sons of the prophets" in verse 35. Grappling with the problems of warfare Ahab called the Israelite elders together for counsel. At this crucial moment an unnamed prophet came with God's message expressing divine concern for the man-God relationship. This prophet promised God's manifestation in mighty acts of deliverance for the purpose that "you shall know that I am the Lord" (v. 13). A second victory over the Syrians was given to Ahab subsequently—again with a divinely revealed interpretation so that "you shall know that I am the Lord" (v. 28). Ahab, however, did not acknowledge these prophets to the extent of asking their advice in time of victory, but made a covenant with Benhadad, king of Syria. Consequently Ahab was warned that he as king as well as his nation would suffer the consequences. Instead of turning to God in repentance, Ahab returned to Samaria embittered and angry (vv. 42–43).

Elijah had one more encounter with Ahab (I Kings 21). After Ahab and Jezebel disregarded the law of inheritance as given in the Mosaic revelation and ignored justice and righteousness in the execution of Naboth, Elijah was commissioned to deliver another message from God to Ahab. The king of Israel was solemnly warned by the prophet that, for his guilt in the stoning of Naboth and his illegal possession of the vineyard, his life would be terminated in such a manner that dogs would lick his blood and that his dynasty would be exterminated. When Ahab temporarily repented, the verdict concerning the extermination of his family was postponed to the next generation.

The final encounter between Ahab and true prophets is vividly portrayed in I Kings 22. Ahab and Jehoshaphat, whose alliance was sealed by the marriage of Jehoram and Athaliah, were about to recapture Ramoth in Gilead from Syrian control. As Jehoshaphat agreed to aid Ahab in this venture, he requested that they should ascertain the "word of the Lord" (v. 5). When four hundred prophets of Ahab unanimously avowed that "the Lord shall deliver it into the hand of the king," Jehoshaphat asked for "a prophet of the Lord," implying that Ahab's prophets were false. When Ahab agreed to call Micaiah, the prophets of Ahab led by Zedekiah unanimously continued their assurance that this military engagement would be successful. Micaiah appeared before the kings and this assembly of prophets with the condition that he would deliver God's message. When Micaiah concurred with the advice given by the prophets, Ahab recognized his mockery and demanded that he should declare to him God's Word. In response Micaiah clearly predicted the death of Ahab and the defeat of Israel. For this Micaiah was imprisoned by Ahab with the order that he not be released until Ahab returned from battle.

Having full knowledge of this divinely revealed message Ahab resorted to his own wisdom. Hoping to avoid identification he disguised himself as he went into battle. Micaiah's prediction, however, was fulfilled when a stray arrow wounded Ahab in battle. Elijah's prediction was likewise fulfilled—the dogs licked the blood of Ahab after he returned to Samaria in his chariot fatally wounded.

PIETY AND TOLERANCE

The Southern Kingdom during the time of Ahab provides a contrast to idolatrous Israel. The man-God relationship was nationally established and maintained through Jehoshaphat (II Chron. 17–20). As king he set the example of seeking after God and sent princes, priests, and Levites throughout the land to instruct the people in the Mosaic message. He was concerned about removing idolatry, although some of the high places were still retained in certain areas. In times of national emergency Jehoshaphat himself stood before his people humbly confessing his dependence upon God and advising his people to believe God's prophets. Personally he reflected considerable knowledge of Israel's history and the Pentateuch in addressing his people. In appointing judges throughout the kingdom, Jehoshaphat reminded them of the essence of the Mosaic revelation which indicated that they should fear or revere God (II Chron. 19:7) and that they should administer their duties as judges according to the principles of justice prescribed by Moses. Cases that could not be solved in the local cities could be brought to Jerusalem where elders, priests, and Levites officiated.

For his ungodly alliances Jehoshaphat was severely rebuked. Returning from participation in Ahab's final battle with the Syrians in which his life was providentially spared, Jehoshaphat was met by the prophet Jehu, the son of Hanani. The king of Judah was solemnly rebuked for helping the ungodly and loving those who hate the Lord (II Chron. 19:1–2). Love for man could only be expressed in the context of a wholehearted love and devotion for God.

Eliezer was another prophet who rebuked Jehoshaphat for his alliance with the wicked Omride dynasty (II Chron. 20:-35–37). The joint naval venture of Jehoshaphat and Ahaziah failed when their ships were wrecked, as had been predicted by this prophet of the Lord.

Elisha also made Jehoshaphat conscious of his association with wicked kings (II Kings 3) when he joined Joram, the son of Ahab, and the king of Edom in war against Mesha, the king of Moab. In desperation when their water supply failed, these kings appealed to Elisha, who happened to be in the Israelite camp. It was Jehoshaphat's request for a prophet through whom inquiry of God could be made that revealed Elisha's presence. Since the king of Israel was in command of this military expedition, Elisha retorted that Joram should consult the prophets of Ahab and Jezebel. Resigned to doom unless divine aid was forthcoming, Joram pleaded with Elisha. The prophet Elisha boldly replied that he would abandon them to their fate were it not for his regard for Jehoshaphat. Then Elisha assured them of the Lord's provision of an adequate water supply and also of a victory over Moab.

The prophetic ministry of Elisha, in which God's mighty acts and messages were made known to Israel in a more extensive manner than through Elijah, began in the days of Ahab and continued for approximately four decades under the dynasty of Jehu. The last recorded confrontation between Elijah and the Omride rulers occurred when Ahaziah, the son of Ahab, sent messengers to Baalzebub, the god of Ekron (II Kings 1). Sent by divine command, Elijah stopped the messengers, predicted that Ahaziah would not recover, and finally appeared in person before the king announcing God's judgment. The fulfillment of this prediction brought Joram, another son of Ahab, to the throne in Israel.

Elisha was very active during the twelve years of Joram's

reign, which ended in judgment as the Omride dynasty, including Jezebel and many Baal zealots, was exterminated. Elisha's fame extended throughout Israel and beyond as he continued teaching in the schools of the prophets founded by Elijah. Through miraculous aid he provided for numerous people in their needs. For a widow he multiplied her oil to redeem her sons from possible enslavement, to the Shunammite woman's son he restored life, and for the sons of the prophets he provided food (II Kings 4). Through Elisha's instructions Naaman, the Syrian captain, secured healing from his leprosy. When one of the students lost his axhead Elisha miraculously recovered it.

Elisha had direct contact with King Joram on numerous occasions. In the war against Moab he boldly chided the king to consult the prophets of Ahab and Jezebel and not to expect help from the prophet of the Lord. When Joram was shaken by the letter from the Syrian king requesting Naaman's healing, Elisha sent word to Joram offering his services so that the Syrian captain might "know that there is a prophet in Israel" (II Kings 5:8). Repeatedly Joram was divinely aided through Elisha's ministry in obtaining relief from the Syrian invaders. Elisha faithfully delivered God's message to Joram frequently making predictions and experiencing their fulfillment.

During Joram's reign Elisha extended his ministry to Damascus, the capital of Syria. When Benhadad, the Syrian king who was suffering from a serious disease, sent his servant Hazael to him to inquire about the prospects for recovery, Elisha informed Hazael that the king would die (II Kings 8:10). Subsequently Hazael became king in accordance with what had been revealed to Elijah at Mount Horeb. Elisha's predictions concerning Hazael's oppressive warfare toward the Israelites were also fulfilled during Hazael's reign in Syria (II Kings 10:32–33; 13:3).

Elisha's final mission involving the Omride dynasty was the anointing of Jehu, a son of Jehoshaphat the son of Nimshi, as the king of Israel (II Kings 9). The explicit message through Elisha

was that the blood of the servants of God who had been martyred by Ahab would be avenged in the extermination of the
royal family together with the Baal zealots. Judgment had been
postponed when Ahab repented in response to Elijah's warning
(I Kings 21). Mercy had been extended in the ministry of Elisha
during Joram's reign but now Jehu was divinely commissioned
to execute judgment. Consequently Elijah's prediction concerning Ahab and Jezebel was fulfilled. Even Ahaziah, the king
of Judah who was grandson of both Ahab and Jehoshaphat, was
killed in this judgment.

Although Elisha lived throughout the reigns of Jehu and
Jehoahaz and died during the rule of Jehoash, *ca.* 798 B.C.,
nothing is recorded about his activity except the circumstances
of his death. The king of Israel was greatly concerned about the
loss of this great prophet.

Both Elijah and Elisha were frequently identified as "the man
of God." Through their messages and miracles they were acknowledged as God's representatives. Active during a period of
excessive apostasy when the royal Omride dynasty was committed to do evil in Israel, these prophets explicitly conveyed God's
revelation through the spoken word and mighty acts. Elisha's
ministry continued for over four decades after the Omride
dynasty was exterminated. Even though Baalism was terminated as the official religion, Jehu failed to provide God-
fearing leadership but continued to influence the Israelites in
idolatrous ways, ignoring the Mosaic revelation (II Kings 10:31).

RELIGIOUS CONFUSION

Godly leadership and a concern for the Word of God were
abruptly terminated in the Southern Kingdom with the death
of Jehoshaphat, *ca.* 848 B.C. The consequences of Jehoshaphat's
alliance with the Omride dynasty, for which he was severely
rebuked by several prophets, came to almost disastrous fruition
in the following decade.

Jehoram, the son of Jehoshaphat, was married to Athaliah, who apparently was wholly devoted to the Baalism promoted by her parents, Jezebel and Ahab. In killing all his brothers Jehoram exemplified his wickedness, which precipitated judgment in the rebellion of Edom through which the king almost lost his life. Warning came to Jehoram through letters from Elijah the prophet (II Chron. 21:12–15). God's message was explicit. Jehoram's bloodshed and his failure to follow the examples of Jehoshaphat and Asa in providing God-fearing leadership and by contrast his promoting of the idolatrous influence of the Omride dynasty precipitated God's judgment. Subsequently all of Jehoram's sons save Ahaziah were killed. For several of the eight years of his reign he suffered from an incurable disease. When he died the people did not mourn his death, nor did they bury him in the tomb of the kings.

The death of Jehoram did not relieve the godless condition in Judah. Ahaziah, son of Jehoram and Athaliah, had ruled only one year when he was killed in Jehu's accession to the throne in Samaria. Athaliah immediately seized the Davidic throne in Jerusalem, attempting to kill all royal heirs as she began her six-year reign of terror. The brothers of Ahaziah had already been taken captive by the Edomites or killed by Jehu in his purge. Joash, an infant son of Ahaziah, however, was saved by Jehosheba, who was a daughter of Jehoram and also the wife of Jehoiada, the high priest. Under Jehoiada's leadership Athaliah was executed and Joash was enthroned at the age of six (II Kings 11; II Chron. 23).

Jehoiada is not identified as a prophet, nor did he claim to have a new message from God. He was concerned about doing the known will of God as revealed in the Mosaic law and in subsequent writings. Known to him was the simple fact that they as God's covenant people were to have a king of the Davidic lineage and a ruler who was concerned about the vital relationship between his people and God instead of promoting idolatrous Baalism. Jehoiada also supervised the destruction of the Baal shrines, organized the Levites for service, and ruled in behalf of Joash until the young king became of age.

As long as Jehoiada lived during the reign of Joash both priest and king were vitally concerned about the man-God relationship. Both exerted leadership in observing the law of Moses, repairing the temple, and replacing genuine worship of God for Baalism. When Jehoiada died, some time after the twenty-third year of Joash's reign, *ca.* 810 B.C., he had gained such recognition for doing "good in Israel, both toward God and toward his house," that he was buried in the city of David among the kings (II Chron. 24:16). After Jehoiada's burial Joash yielded to the pressure of some of his princes in permitting them to break the commandments by substituting idolatry for their devotion to God.

Except for Zechariah, the son of Jehoiada (II Chron. 24:19–20), the prophets who testified against these idolatrous leaders are not identified. Empowered by the Spirit of God, this prophet warned that God was forsaking them. Because of this warning, Zechariah was stoned by the princes who influenced the king to issue a decree for execution. The prophet was martyred with the prayer that God would execute vengeance.

King Hazael of Syria was used toward the end of the ninth century to fulfill the prediction made through Elisha (II Kings 8:7–15). Frequently he attacked Jehu and Jehoahaz, devastating the Northern Kingdom east of Jordan as far south as the Arnon Valley (II Kings 10:32–33). Shortly after Zechariah was martyred, the Syrian armies captured Gath and advanced to Jerusalem (II Kings 12:17–18). In desperation Joash sent temple and palace treasures to Hazael to avert a Syrian occupation of Jerusalem. However, a small Syrian army humiliated Judah in executing judgment as the prediction made by Zechariah the prophet was fulfilled.

Baalism, after permeating Israel and Judah, left both kingdoms in a very weakened condition. Revolutions in the north in 841 B.C. and in the south in 835 B.C. provided the opportune time for Syrian expansion. During the rest of the ninth century, Syria under its powerful king, Hazael, extended its domination into Judah as well as Israel.

RELIEF AND RECOVERY

Relief came to both kingdoms in the death of Hazael, the Syrian king, who had repeatedly exacted tribute, captives, and territory from the kings ruling in Jerusalem and Samaria. Although Elisha outlived Hazael there is no mention of his activities during the reigns of Jehu and Jehoahaz, *ca.* 841–798 B.C. Release from oppression in answer to the prayer of Jehoahaz (II Kings 13:3–4) may have come with the termination of Hazael's reign, *ca.* 801 B.C. The next king of Israel, Jehoash, expressed genuine concern when he realized that Elisha was on his deathbed. Elisha had an encouraging prediction for the king, assuring him of three victories over the Syrian oppressors (II Kings 13:-14–25). This was fulfilled when Jehoash recaptured Israelite cities from the control of Benhadad, the new king in Syria.

Two unnamed prophets delivered pertinent messages to King Amaziah which were crucial to Judah in its effort to regain national strength as Syrian power waned (II Chron. 25). Amaziah was very suddenly enthroned after his father Joash had been wounded by Syrian invaders and assassinated by his servants. As soon as Amaziah was well enough established he mustered an army of three hundred thousand men to resubjugate Edom which had revolted under Jehoram (II Kings 8:20). After Amaziah hired one hundred thousand additional soldiers from Jehoash, the king of Israel, a man of God advised him not to enlist the aid of apostate Israel. In addition he assured the king that God's provision would more than duplicate the military aid as well as the price he had paid the king of Israel. With his own army Amaziah defeated Edom.

Upon his return from this decisive victory Amaziah introduced Edomite idolatry into Judah. Subsequently another man of God came to warn Amaziah against breaking God's commandments by bowing to idols. When Amaziah defied this prophet, God's judgment came upon the king through his unwise policy toward Jehoash whose soldiers had pillaged cities after they had been dismissed by Amaziah. In a challenged battle between the north and the south, Amaziah was not only defeated, but Jerusalem was plundered, and he was taken as a prisoner. Fifteen years later he was restored to his throne. Thus the prophecy of this man of God was fulfilled. These developments left Judah in a weakened condition and much inferior to the Northern Kingdom, in spite of the victory over Edom.

JONAH—GOD'S MERCY TO GENTILES

The prophet Jonah was active in the post-Elisha era. It may have been during Jeroboam's co-regency with his father (ca. 793–781 B.C.) that Jonah made the prediction about this king of Israel (II Kings 14:25–27). In subsequent years Jeroboam II (793–753 B.C.) reconquered the territory Israel had previously lost to Hazael and led the Northern Kingdom to an unprecedented peak of political and economic prosperity.

Jonah's mission to Nineveh may be dated in the reign of Assyrian king Adad-Nirari II (810–783 B.C.) or Assurdan III (771–754 B.C.). The account of Jonah's adventures as given in the book bearing his name was probably written by him. Jonah's experience explicitly teaches that God is merciful to heathen nations when they repent. The plagues in Nineveh in 765 and 759 B.C. and the total eclipse of the sun on June 15, 763, probably conditioned the Assyrians for the message of judgment announced by Jonah. The teaching in Israelite law and history that God responded in mercy to those who repent was vividly illustrated in Jonah's life as it applied to the sinful city of Nineveh. His experience had prophetic significance as indicated by Jesus Christ (Matt. 12:40).

Whereas the people of Nineveh repented and turned to God, the Israelites refused to heed the warnings by the prophets during the eighth century. In view of the impending judgment both Amos and Hosea forthrightly admonished their people to repent, abandon their idolatry, and turn to God.

AMOS—ISRAEL CONFRONTED BY GOD

Amos came as a divinely called prophet on a preaching mission to the Northern Kingdom in the reign of Jeroboam II, probably during the last decade of his kingship (*ca.* 760–750 B.C.). The man-God relationship permeates his entire message. His appeal to the Israelites is based on their covenant with God and a reminder that they are failing to live up to the requirements expected in this relationship. The repeated references to the law of love for God and for fellow men seem to indicate that they had the Mosaic law as given in the Pentateuch but were neglecting to relate it to daily life. Frequently the history of Israel came into focus as Amos reminded them of God's dealings with them in the past.

Although the message of Amos is given in the Northern Kingdom with application to the particular situation prevailing there, the divine perspective is universal. The temple on Mount Zion is the point at which God enters into the affairs of mankind (1:2). Israel as a whole is God's covenant people. Although Judah is included with the surrounding nations, there are several additional references which indicate that Judah and Israel are regarded as one in the covenantal relationship with God. The political division is temporal. Judgment is coming to each of the two kingdoms, but ultimately they will be restored as one nation under David (9:11–15).

Amos has relatively little in his message that is new. Taking into account the prevailing social, religious, and political conditions, Amos reminds the Israelites of their sins and predicts coming judgment and restoration. Both national and international history are reflected in the appeal Amos makes to the Israelites.

God's dealings with the surrounding nations in their relationship with Israel are not unique with Amos. When God chose Israel, He dealt with the various nations through Israel, judging Egypt for her oppression (Exod. 4–14), defeating the Amalekites in their attack on Israel (Exod. 17), sparing the Edomites, Moabites, and Ammonites (Deut. 2) but destroying the Amorites and other nations in Canaan whose iniquities had reached the point of judgment in God's economy (Deut. 3:21–22). Amos makes the truth relevant to his generation.

Amos introduces his message to Israel with the announcement that God's judgment is coming upon the surrounding nations because of their offense against Israel (1:3–2:5). Syria, with its capital at Damascus, will be punished for her oppression of Israel in the days of Hazael. The Philistines have sold the Israelites as slaves to the Edomites. The Phoenicians are guilty of taking advantage of Israel in their agreements with Edom. The Edomites will be punished for pursuing the Israelites with the sword. The Ammonites are guilty of cruel warfare against Israel and the Moabites have desecrated the tombs of the Edomite kings. The people of Judah have rejected the law through disobedience, have hardened their hearts, and have sinned as their forefathers had done. Amos specifically predicts the destruction by fire of the palaces and forts at Jerusalem.

Israel, however, is due for greater punishment. The reasons are clearly developed. God's grace and goodness had been extended to them in deliverance from Egypt (2:10; 3:1–2, 7), in giving them possession of Canaan (2:9–10), in sending them Nazirites and prophets to warn them (2:11–12), and in sending them drought, famine, crop failure, plagues, and warfare (4:-6–11). The Israelites did not respond to these acts of mercy divinely intended to make them God-conscious.

The admonition to love God and fellow men was disregarded by the Israelites in their total pattern of living. Lacking a genuine love for God they were guilty of idolatry and social evils which reflected their failure to love their fellow men. Against the background of Deuteronomy 1–6, Amos denounces the idolatry prevailing at Gilgal, Bethel, Beersheba, Samaria, Dan, and throughout the land of God's covenant people (3:14; 4:4; 5:5–6; 7:9; 8:14). Their devotion to God and worship according to the law is insincere and hypocritical (4:5; 5:21–23; 6:5). They are taking advantage of their fellow men, which was forbidden in the law wherein they were explicitly taught that God was righteous (Deut. 10:17–19). Therefore righteous judgment must reign among the people (Deut. 29:14–21). Justice should prevail in the courts (Lev. 19:35–36; Deut. 16:18–20) and not partiality (Deut. 1:16–17). Amos asserts that the Israelites accept bribes and sell the poor for a pair of shoes (2:6–7; 4:1; 8:8). Injustice prevails and social evils abound (5:10–12). Cheating in weights is practiced by the merchants (8:5). Practical religion involves both wholehearted devotion to God and love for one's neighbor. Neither the worship of God nor the consideration of one's fellow man can be neglected in the daily pattern of life.

In addition the Israelites had not heeded God's warnings. They caused the Nazirites to break their vows by drinking wine. They silenced the prophets (2:12). Even Amos was rebuked by Amaziah, a priest at Bethel, who reported to King Jeroboam that Amos was a traitor (7:10–17). Honest judges and those who spoke with integrity were hated (5:10).

Israel's failure to live up to the moral requirements of a God who is perfect in righteousness as had been prescribed in the Torah naturally precipitated judgment. The sovereign God who brought the nations under judgment also brought punishment upon Israel. Moses had warned the Israelites that God's judgment upon other nations for their sinfulness would come upon them if they sinned (Lev. 18:24–30; Deut. 9:4). On the other hand, Amos repeatedly emphasizes that the Israelites should prepare to meet God and seek Him (4:12; 5:6, 14–15). That God would be merciful to those who love God wholeheartedly was explicitly stated by Moses in his address to Israel (Deut. 4:29–31).

Amos admonished them to place their trust in God, not in

themselves or in their idols. Foolishly they pride themselves on their own power (6:13). Their false glory, their manpower, their beautiful homes, and their cities will all be destroyed.

Amos reminds the Israelites of what God is like even as Moses had done in his generation (Exod. 19–24; Deut. 4–6). God is the God of all nations and chose Israel as His particular interest (Amos 1:1–3:2). God is omnipotent, controlling all nature and then determining famine and plenty (4:1–13; 5:8). God is omniscient in knowing their thoughts (4:13). He is also a God of mercy (4:11; 7:1–6). Since the relationship between God and His wayward people had been so explicitly delineated in Deuteronomy 4:25ff., Amos emphasizes these attributes of God to correct the Israelites' erroneous ideas about Him. Amos also points out that they have not revered God but have profaned His name by immorality (2:7), and have silenced the prophets (2:12). This is the God they should acknowledge in their pattern of living as they prepare to meet Him (4:12).

God's mercy and judgment are vividly portrayed in five visions. Destruction of the surrounding nations is graphically described as a devastation by fire. When God shares with Amos His intent to send swarms of locusts or fire to destroy Israel, the prophet responds with intercession. Mercy is extended and judgment delayed (7:1–6). The third vision portrays God's inspection of Israel and the issuing of the warning that judgment is inevitable (7:7–9). Death was the penalty prescribed by Moses for idolatry (Deut. 7:4). The fourth vision indicates that judgment is near (8:1–2). The fifth vision (9:1–6) depicts the thorough destruction God sends in which no one in earth or heaven will escape.

The predictions concerning Israel's destruction are extensive and detailed. The dynasty of Jeroboam will be destroyed by the sword (7:9). This was fulfilled in 753 B.C., when Zechariah, Jeroboam's son, was killed after a six-month reign (II Kings 15:8–12). The nation will be subjected to an enemy invasion (3:11), which will come from the north and oppress Israel (6:14). Idols and idol shrines will be destroyed (3:14; 7:9). Idolaters will never rise again (8:14). The beautiful homes and palaces they have built will be leveled (6:8–11) and the people will be exiled beyond Damascus (5:27). That this national fate was imminent is indicated in the specific prediction Amos makes concerning Amaziah, the Bethel priest who opposed him (7:17). Amaziah and his children will be killed, his wife will commit adultery, and the Israelites will be taken into captivity. The imminence of their judgment was emphasized through the vision of the basket of summer fruit. Amos also predicts a future famine of God's Word (8:11–13). The predictions of invasion, destruction, and captivity were fulfilled in the coming of the Assyrians, beginning in 745 B.C., who terminated the independence of Syria in 732 and the Northern Kingdom of Israel in 722 B.C.

Like the prophets before him, Amos had a message of hope, which is introduced in the last chapter of the book, where he emphasizes that no one will escape God's judgment. The sinful kingdom will be rooted up and all sinners will perish, but a remnant in Israel will be saved, as indicated by God's use of a sieve. In accordance with the assurance in the Mosaic revelation that God's covenant is eternal and the subsequent promise that God's throne will be established forever, Amos offers the hope that the Davidic kingdom will be restored and raised to a place of superiority over other nations. The fortunes of Israel will be restored so that the people will build cities and inhabit them and enjoy the crops of their vineyards. This prediction (9:11–15) was still awaiting fulfillment when the Jerusalem council convened at the beginning of the Christian era (Acts 15:16–17).

HOSEA—GOD'S LOVE PORTRAYED

The prophet Hosea likewise expressed a genuine concern about Israel's relationship with God. His ministry began before the reign of Jehu's dynasty was violently terminated in 753 and continued into or even beyond the reign of Hoshea (732–722 B.C.), when overtures were made to Egypt for help against Assyria as is reflected in chapter 7. Consequently his messages were given over a period of three or more decades. Although Hosea may have extended his ministry beyond the fall of Samaria, his book might have been published before the siege of Samaria began in 725 B.C.

Considerable light is shed upon the state of the Northern Kingdom by Hosea. Idolatrous worship and immoral practices were prevalent at various sanctuaries (2:5, 8, 16; 3:1; 4:12–14; 17–18; 10:5–6; 13:2). Lying, perjury, murder, stealing, debauchery, and bloodshed were common (4:1–2; 6:8; 7:1, 5–7; 10:4; 12:7–8). The priests and rulers were guilty of ensnaring and deluding the people in the ways of idolatry (5:1).

The message of love is more elaborately portrayed through Hosea than by any other prophet. This emphasis to apostate Israel in the closing decades of its existence as a kingdom should have made the generation which was about to be absorbed by the Assyrians conscious of God's extended mercy. In deed and in word Hosea communicated to them God's love and pleaded with them to renew their covenant with God.

According to Moses' exposition of the law to the congregation of Israel before his death, love was the keystone in a vital relationship between God and Israel. God's love was expressed in the choosing of the patriarchs and their descendants (Deut. 4:37). Because of this love, God's power was demonstrated in the deliverance of the Israelites from Egypt and therefore Moses admonished the Israelites to acknowledge God (Deut. 4:39) and to love Him (Deut. 6:5). This wholehearted love would find practical expression in a reverence and fear of God which would result in the obeying of His commandments. Since the teaching and observance of the law as well as the experience of learning to fear God was to be taught in the home, this relationship of love became an individual matter (Deut. 6:1–25). Love between God and Israel was essential for the maintenance of the covenant (Deut. 7:6–15). God promised that His love with all its benefits would continue upon those who exhibited a practical expression of love for Him in obeying His commandments (Deut. 10:12–11:31).

Through his marriage and the naming of his children, Hosea vividly illustrated to the Israelites God's love, which continues even though they do not love Him. The birth of his first son, named Jezreel, precipitated the announcement that God would terminate the Jehu dynasty and the independence of the Northern Kingdom. The name of the second child, Lo-ruhamah, signified that God would be withdrawing His mercy. When the third child was born and named Lo-ammi, Hosea announced that God was disowning His people Israel. When Hosea's wife, Gomer, became disloyal and left him, the message of the prophet was applied to Israel's loving relationship with God. Even as Gomer ignored Hosea and lived an immoral life, so Israel had disregarded God through her disloyalty and had turned to sinful ways. Yet, as long as Hosea was active, God's love and mercy continued so that he appealed to them to repent before the coming judgment. Thus his message is crucially relevant.

Hosea explicitly depicts Israel's basic problem. People and priest have rejected the covenant and the law (8:1). The knowledge of God is not among them because they have rejected or nullified this vital relationship and have failed to incorporate the terms of the covenant in their daily lives. Because of the lack of this knowledge they will be destroyed (4:1–11). The knowledge essential for Israel had been revealed in the law and the terms of the covenant. God had made known to Israel His plan (5:9), and the knowledge of God was more important than sacrifice (6:6). An act of involvement, commitment to God by the whole person, was essential as stressed by Moses (Deut. 6:5). This inner dedication to God involved mind, heart, thought, and emotion rather than mere dedication to ceremonies.

The word "know" is used repeatedly by Hosea in his effort to

communicate clearly. When he points out that Israel did not
know that God provided the crops (2:8), he conveys the important fact that they are not living in accordance with this realization. That God was the sustainer of the universe, providing
crops and all material benefits, was known to them through
previous revelation. Now they use these crops to make sacrifice
to idols. The divine promise is that in the future they shall
"know" the Lord (2:20), meaning that they shall sincerely serve
Him. Likewise in 11:3 the word "know" signifies realization.
Intellectually they were conscious of the fact that God had
delivered them from Egypt but they did not act in accordance
with this knowledge, ignoring their benefactor. Likewise "I did
know you in the wilderness" (13:5) indicates that God manifested His power in behalf of Israel. The context of the other
references (5:3–4; 6:3) also supports the fact that "know" means
practical realization of knowledge that is reflected in daily conduct.

Rejection of God's Word and the failure to acknowledge God
resulted in the terrible conditions that prevailed (4:1–13).
Truth, mercy, and the knowledge of God had been replaced
with swearing, lying, killing, stealing, and adultery. The priests
were guilty of forgetting the law and of approving the sins of
the people. Consequently the people were consulting wooden
objects used for divination. They were resorting to idolatrous
shrines instead of turning to their God. They mingled with the
heathen and adopted their ways. The rulers were so sinful that
they did not realize that their strength was failing (7:1–10).
Instead of turning to God they looked to Egypt and Assyria for
help.

Hosea warns them of coming judgment. After the initial announcement of God's judgment in chapter 1 he foretells crop
failure and famine (2:1–13). Destruction is coming because the
people have failed to keep the law and the covenant (8:1–14).
God will terminate His love for them and they shall be scattered
among the nations because they have not responded to His

gracious dealings with them (9:1–17). God's judgment is sure to come (13:1–3). Samaria must bear her guilt (13:16).

Certain that judgment will come, Hosea offers throughout his sermons a hope of restoration. His messages of coming destruction summarized in chapter 1 include the hope of Israel's regathering (1:10–11). In contrast to the impending destruction and the abandonment of their land to the wild beasts, Hosea assures them of a future state of absolute peace extending even to the animal world (2:14–23), when Israel in reality will be God's people. God's judgment will ultimately be followed by a regathering of His people (11:10). They will be ransomed from the power of death (13:14). God will heal their backsliding and Israel shall no more turn to idols (14:4–9).

Hosea, as God's messenger, is keenly conscious of the fact that God's mercy still prevails as long as he is among them as God's commissioned messenger to warn them. Consequently he makes numerous appeals to his people Israel. He admonishes them to return to God and assures them of God's restoration (6:1–3). If they will plant seeds of righteousness they will reap a crop of God's love and mercy. Theirs is the responsibility to seek after God, since they have been cultivating wickedness and raising crops of sin (10:12–13). Hosea is conscious of God's compassion and love for Israel. In chapter 11 his emphasis shifts from matrimonial love to the compassionate love of a father for his son. God has been a father to Israel, teaching the Israelites to walk, delivering them from Egyptian bondage, and nurturing them in the land of Canaan. Although they are determined to desert God, they will not be completely abandoned in judgment even though this judgment is certain (13:16).

The condition on which God's mercy can be obtained is repentance and confession of sin (14:1–3). By expressing their complete confidence in God through a wholehearted commitment and acknowledging that their trust in Assyria and in their idols is futile, they can renew their covenant with God. This advice was in conformity with that which Moses had prescribed in the book of Deuteronomy. God would respond in mercy to restore them if they repented.

Hosea's warnings were not sufficiently heeded to avert judgment. The prediction that the Northern Kingdom would terminate was fulfilled in 722 B.C. as the Assyrians reduced this kingdom to a province. The Israelites had failed to heed God's law as well as the warnings of the prophets that were sent to them (II Kings 17).

ISAIAH—JUDGMENT AND THE GOSPEL OF LOVE

For more than a half century, while four Assyrian kings advanced their conquering armies across the land God had given to the Israelites as their possession, Isaiah was called to proclaim the gospel divinely revealed through Moses. He began his ministry in 740 B.C., five years after Tiglath-pileser III of Assyria initiated a military policy of subduing nationalism by removing conquered populations from their homelands to distant parts of his empire. The citizens of both kingdoms had reason to fear the realistic threat of conquest and occupation by the powerful Assyrians. Consequently Isaiah had much to say about these developments during his ministry as God's messenger to an apostate people.

In the year of Isaiah's call to the prophetic ministry, Uzziah —who had withstood Assyrian aggression—died. Jotham, who maintained his father's anti-Assyrian policy, was replaced on the Davidic throne by Ahaz in 736/35 B.C. The latter championed peace and friendship with the Assyrians. Simultaneously Pekah of Israel and Rezin of Syria formed an alliance to oppose the powerful Assyrians who were then consolidating conquests northward into Urartu. Realizing that Ahaz did not support them in their anti-Assyrian policy, Pekah and Rezin declared war on him hoping that they could conquer Judah before they faced the Assyrians coming from the north.

Precisely when the news of this declaration of war reached Jerusalem, Isaiah confronted Ahaz with God's message (7:1ff.) In this crucial situation the king of Judah was advised to trust in God and was assured that the two invading kings would be dethroned within a few years. Ahaz, however, ignored Isaiah and sent tribute to the Assyrians, appealing for aid (II Kings 16:7ff.). Isaiah boldly warned Ahaz that God would summon Assyria like a bee or use Assyria like a razor (7:18–20) to subject Judah to the ravages of war.

The appeal of Ahaz to Tiglath-pileser III was temporarily very successful in spite of Isaiah's warnings. Rezin was killed as the Assyrians occupied Damascus in 732. Samaria was spared conquest for a decade after Pekah was assassinated and replaced by Hoshea. Ahaz met the Assyrian king in Damascus and subsequently built an altar in Jerusalem and arranged other temple furnishings in deference to the king of Assyria (II Kings 16:10–18). Isaiah continued to warn about impending developments. The Assyrians in time would advance through Palestine like a river and submerge Judah to the neck (8:5–8). Speaking of the futility of the plan of Ahaz the prophet asserted that friendship with Assyria would not save Judah when the raging flood (28:9–22) would surge through the land. God was using Assyria as a rod to punish Judah (10:5).

Against this background in which a defiant godless king is ruling from the throne of David, Isaiah offers a message of hope for the God-fearing people. Veiled in somewhat ambiguous language is the announcement that a child will be born whose name will be Immanuel, meaning "God with us" (7:14). While this was a hopeful promise to the people of God, it communicated a threat to Ahaz in the possibility of his replacement. The birth of a son is promised whose equality with God is recognized in the identification as "mighty God," who will establish an everlasting kingdom (9:6–7). In Zion provision will be made so that those who place their faith in this individual will not be disappointed (28:16), as the generation associated with Ahaz will be when they see their plans shattered. The future hopes for a righteous ruler and a kingdom in which justice and peace prevail universally are delineated by Isaiah in chapter 11. Ultimately God's people will be regathered from the lands to which they will have been scattered in divine judgment (chaps. 24–27, 35).

In the days of Hezekiah, 716–686 B.C., Isaiah was deeply involved in the Judah–Assyrian relations. After Samaria was conquered in 722 B.C., reducing the Northern Kingdom to an Assyrian province, Sargon II continued the victorious advance southward. For three years Isaiah appeared publicly on the streets of Jerusalem in sparsely clad attire to warn the people of Judah not to interfere with the Assyrian siege of Ashdod, *ca.* 711 B.C. (20:1–6).

Following Sennacherib's enthronement in Nineveh in 705 the Assyrians continued their conquest of Palestine. By 701 Hezekiah, who already had paid vast amounts of tribute, was given an ultimatum to surrender to the Assyrian king. Isaiah reassured Hezekiah that Jerusalem would not be conquered by the Assyrians (chaps. 36–37). Even though Sennacherib boasted in his annals that he conquered forty-six walled cities and took two hundred thousand captives from Palestine, Hezekiah and the people of Jerusalem were miraculously delivered from the Assyrian army as Isaiah had predicted throughout his ministry.

The message of Isaiah's preaching mission to the Israelites is summarized in chapters 1–5. His basic indictment against God's chosen nation is that they have broken their relationship with God (1:1–31). Instead of loving and serving God wholeheartedly they have ignored God whose charge against them is:

> They have revolted against me.

Observing their iniquity and corrupt pattern of living Isaiah asserts that

They have abandoned the Lord
They have despised the Holy One of Israel
They have turned away from him.

All their religious activities—offerings and sacrifices, solemn assemblies and appointed feasts—are unacceptable to God as long as they mistreat their neighbors. Instead of demonstrating love for their fellow men they are guilty of oppressing the poor and neglecting the widows and orphans. Injustice permeates the society in Isaiah's generation. Consequently God's word is that

Zion shall be redeemed by justice
And those in her who repent, by righteousness.
Rebels and sinners alike shall be crushed
And those who forsake the Lord shall perish.

Even as an owner destroys a vineyard that does not produce fruit, so God will bring judgment upon Judah in due time (5:-1–30). In contrast to the devastation that will come upon Judah's capital, the divine assurance is given that the time is coming when God will restore Zion as a universal center from which

He shall judge between the nations
And impose terms on many peoples;
And they shall beat their swords into plowshares
And their spears into pruning hooks;
One nation shall not raise the sword against another,
Nor shall they train for war again (2:4–5).

After Hezekiah had withstood the Assyrian pressure triumphantly and had recovered from his serious illness, a delegation from Babylon came to congratulate him on his recovery. When Isaiah heard that Hezekiah had shown them his treasury as well as his armory, he rebuked the king with the prediction that his descendants would be taken into Babylonian captivity (39:1–8).

With the divinely imparted knowledge that his people will be exiled to Babylon, Isaiah unfolds the most extensive delineation

of God's love for his people who are subjected to divine judgment because of their idolatry (chaps. 40–56). Israel was divinely chosen as a nation to be God's servant for the purpose of
bringing salvation to the Gentile nations. Because of her idolatry and sinful ways the condition of Israel is pathetically portrayed in chapter 42:19:

> Who is blind but my servant?
> Who is so deaf as my messenger whom I send?
> But this is a people plundered and despoiled
> They have become a prey with none to deliver them.

Although Israel in this condition cannot accomplish God's purpose for which they have been chosen, God's attitude toward
them is one of compassion and concern even though they have
sinned (43:4ff.):

> Because you are precious in my eyes
> And glorious because I love you
> I will give men in exchange for you,
> Fear not I am with you.
> You are my witnesses
> My servants whom I have chosen.

God, who is omnipotent and has created Israel, asserts that
He will not give His glory to another nor His praise to idols
(42:8). Deliverance from Babylonian exile is promised through
Cyrus His anointed (45:1).

Deliverance from sin is also divinely promised. Even though
they wearied God with their crime and iniquities, God in His
concern for them gives the assurance (43:25) that

> I even I am the one who wipes out your transgressions
>   for my own sake,
> I will not remember your sins.

And again in 44:21ff.:

Remember this, O Jacob
you, Israel are my servant
I have formed you to be my servant
O Israel you will never be forgotten by me.

So precious is Israel to God that He asserts in 49:16:

I have inscribed you on the palms of my hand.

Although God had promised to blot out their sin (44:22-23) this forgiveness could be provided only through vicarious suffering. Israel—subjected to shame and reproach in Babylonian exile, possibly suffering a double measure—did not suffer innocently but was there because of her sin and apostasy (40:2). Their suffering—no matter how excessive—could not provide salvation for others. Israel herself needed someone to atone for them. Through divine provision a Servant emerged (49:1-7) to

restore Israel to God
be a light to the nations
so that
my salvation may reach to earth's farthest bounds.

Although this Servant of rulers will be despised and rejected by mankind, he will ultimately be given recognition by kings, and princes will prostrate before him.

It is this Servant who is portrayed in chapter 53 as the one who suffers for others. Unlike Israel, who had broken their relationship with God through idolatry, this Servant possesses righteousness. Through this righteous Servant—the last reference to the word "servant" in the singular in Isaiah—provision is made for many to be made righteous.

The salvation provided through this Servant is the heritage of the servants of the Lord (54:17). This salvation is delineated in chapter 55 and the appeal or invitation is crystal clear:

Let men cast off their wicked deeds
Let them banish from their minds the very thought of

> doing wrong.
> Let them turn to the Lord
>> that he may have mercy on them
> And to our God
>> for he will abundantly pardon.

This invitation is issued to the nations as well as to the Israelites (56:1–8). Strangers, eunuchs, foreigners, gentiles—all are invited

> to be his servants . . .
> For my house shall be called a house of prayer for all nations.

The reality of this salvation provided for the individual who responds is in essence the same as delineated by Moses in his appeal to the Israelite to love God with all his heart. The man-God relationship is basic. In reality God does not dwell among a people who practice injustice and worship idols (57:1–13) but God does reside within the individual who is

> contrite and lowly in spirit
> to revive the spirit of the humble (57:15).

When a holy God resides in the heart of an individual, an ethical dimension is injected into the total pattern of living.

Who can appeal to God and be assured of an answer? It is the person who expresses love and concern for his neighbor in daily life (58:1–14). External religion expressed in fasting and rituals is futile when the homeless, the poor, and the hungry are neglected. But the one who demonstrated love for his fellow men can experience the divine guidance continually and his life will be like a spring of water. This will result in a life similar to that which Jesus later portrayed in speaking about the Holy Spirit residing in the individual (John 7:37–39).

As Isaiah delineates the reality of injustice and the prevailing social evils (59:1ff.), he confirms again the previous predictions (cf. chaps. 2; 11–12; 24–27; 35) that the glory of Zion will be restored. The Lord will once more reestablish Jerusalem and make it the pride and praise of all the earth (chaps. 60–62). In the meantime while injustice, hypocrisy and social inequity prevail among mankind, the divine promise is for the individuals who are identified as God's servants. They will inherit new heavens and a new earth (chaps. 63–66). Note the divine identification of these individuals:

This is the one whom I approve
The lowly and afflicted man who trembles at my word (66:2).

In this manner Isaiah stresses anew for his generation the importance of responding to God's love and of demonstrating this love to one's neighbor.

IX

DIVINE JUDGMENT
AND THE PROMISE

The Southern Kingdom endured several decades of idolatry and bloodshed under the apostate Davidic ruler Manasseh, who probably was responsible for the martyrdom of Isaiah. While the Assyrians extended their conquest through Palestine to some five hundred miles along the river Nile to Thebes, the kingdom of Judah survived even though Manasseh was subjected to temporary exile (II Chron. 33:1–20). During the last half of the seventh century the Assyrian power declined, finally capitulating to the Median and Babylonian coalition when Nineveh was razed in 612 B.C.

For about four decades, 640–609 B.C., optimism prevailed as the outstanding God-fearing king Josiah led his kingdom in a religious revival that extended throughout Judah and Israel. Many undoubtedly hoped that the judgment as announced by Isaiah would be averted.

JEREMIAH—MERCY BEFORE JUDGMENT

Jeremiah—divinely called to the prophetic ministry in 627—warned of impending doom for Jerusalem for forty years as he witnessed revival, reformation, and the disintegration of the kingdom to the point of utter destruction under Zedekiah in

586 B.C. As long as Josiah lived, Jeremiah had freedom to warn the citizens of Judah without being persecuted. However, the sudden death of the thirty-nine-year-old king resulted in adverse circumstances for Jeremiah as he boldly reminded his fellow citizens that Jerusalem would be destroyed in that generation. So intense was his warning during this period of extended mercy that hopes for the restoration explicitly promised are given brief consideration.

The core of Israel's problem, says Jeremiah, is cultic apostasy: they have forsaken God (2:13). More than any other prophet, Jeremiah speaks of this broken relationship with God. Repeatedly he enumerates substitutions that have been made for the wholehearted commitment and love emphasized by Moses. Having forsaken God who is the fountain of living waters, they have hewn out cisterns which are broken and can hold no water.

Israel has ignored God's love which was lavished upon her in her redemption from Egypt and her settlement in Canaan and has sinned in turning to idolatry. The priests have failed in leading the people back to God; the teachers of the law have no vital relationship or contact with God; the rulers themselves are transgressors; and prophets, instead of representing God, are identified with Baal and idolatry. Israel has been divorced from her God. The people lack the fear and reverence for God they should exemplify as His holy people. They have failed to love God and consequently have failed to love their fellow man. All other laws are insignificant when love for God and neighbor is neglected.

Can divorced Israel renew her vows with her God? Jeremiah sees his people plunging toward judgment. In a graphic description the prophet warns his people that God's judgment is certain and imminent. Although he warns them to repent, he realizes that this divine judgment is coming very soon (4:5–6:30).

This broken relationship with God had led to numerous irregularities in their daily pattern of living (7:1–11:23). Legalism, religious formalism, and ritualistic observance of the law seemed to be the order of the day. From Jeremiah's messages it is apparent that Israel trusted in the temple, confident that God would not permit His holy place of worship to be destroyed (7:1). The people were certain that as custodians of the law they were safe (8:8). Presumptively they counted on God's covenant with them, but Jeremiah boldly charged them with their failure in obeying the terms of this relationship. Pointing to the ruins of Shiloh, where the tabernacle was located in the days of Joshua and Eli, he warned that Jerusalem would be subjected to the same fate.

The law in the hands of the scribes and priests has been misused. The external formalities in worship and service can never save them from judgment. While the people ritualistically worship God in the temple, they simultaneously worship idols everywhere—idols so numerous that they have one for each street in Jerusalem and one for each city in the kingdom of Judah.

True religion is lacking. Not knowing God and not exhibiting a wholehearted love for Him, they are far from demonstrating God's love to their fellow men (9:2-7). Instead of loving their neighbors, the generation of Jeremiah's time is guilty of sins of the tongue: slander, lies, deceitfulness, and crafty cunning. Falsehood instead of faithfulness is the law of the land. Through cheating and trickery they take advantage of each other. Oppression is prevalent. There is no such thing as neighborly love. They have no desire to reform their conduct. Greediness, injustice, immorality, murder, and theft are so commonly practiced among them that the offenders feel no shame. Immorality is a concomitant with idolatry (5:1-9; 7:3-11; 23:10-14) for Jeremiah's generation. Moral corruption is inescapable when the fear of God and reverence for His laws are eliminated.

The religious leaders composed of priests and prophets supported the populace in opposition to Jeremiah and the Mosaic revelation. Jeremiah was stunned and horrified that the prophets prophesied falsely and the priests taught according to their own standards with the popular support of the people (5:30–31). With the religious leaders guilty of greediness and deceit falsely assuring the people of peace (6:13–14), misinterpreting the law (8:8–12), misleading the people by claiming to prophesy in God's name (14:13–16), and living in sinful conditions comparable to those of Sodom and Gomorrah, it was apparent that judgment must come (23:9–40). Jeremiah was heartbroken about this condition even though the people repeatedly countered his message as he continued to warn them.

With the temple and Jerusalem about to be destroyed, Jeremiah pressed the importance of each individual's moral and spiritual relationship with God. Confidence should not be fixed in the temple, sacrifices, the priesthood, the ark which symbolized God's presence, knowledge of the law, circumcision, or the covenant. Jeremiah did not oppose the observance of the rites and ceremonies prescribed by the law but, like Moses in Deuteronomy 10:16 and 30:6, he insisted that circumcision of the heart (4:4; 9:26) is essential for those who love God wholeheartedly. Knowledge of the written law is useless unless the law is inscribed on the heart. An inward faith in God, a profound reverence for His law, and a willing obedience expressed in love and devotion—these were essential features of a religion pleasing to God.

With clarity Jeremiah delineates between the individual who pleases God and the person whom God rejects (17:1–18). Sin, engraved on the horns of the altar, is but an expression of what is in the heart of man, the heart being the center and fountainhead of life. The outward actions—treachery, deceit, idolatry, hypocrisy, and all the sins so frequently pinpointed by Jeremiah —are but the fruits or outward expression of a deceitful and corrupt heart. The verdict is that any individual who has confidence in himself and turns away from God is cursed. Like a tree in the desert he has no hopeful prospects for the future. The heart is the source of sin. Judgment in destruction and captivity is inevitable. Those who trust in man instead of in God will ultimately be put to shame.

By contrast the man pleasing to God is the individual who places his confidence or trust in Him. A wholehearted commitment, faith, and love directed Godward instead of toward sinful self will result in fruitfulness throughout the difficulties of life. Like a tree with a good water source, which bears fruit even in times of drought, so the individual, whose trust and confidence is in God, will prosper.

Although Jeremiah was moved to tears as destruction and captivity neared reality, he prayed earnestly, hoping judgment would be postponed or averted. God, however, repeatedly commanded him not to pray—it was too late for prayer. The time had come that Moses (Exod. 32:11; Num. 14:13–20) and Samuel (I Sam. 7:9; 12:23)—conspicuous examples of the power of intercessory prayer—would save themselves only through prayer. Jeremiah's celibacy was to serve as a continual reminder to the people that judgment was coming during his lifetime.

As the Judean kingdom disintegrated under the encroaching advance of the Babylonians, Jeremiah specifically projected the hope for those in exile as it related to their questions and problems. Shortly after some Judean hostages were taken captive to Babylon in 605 B.C., Jeremiah provided a realistic hope in the assurance that after seventy years the captives would return (chap. 25). Speaking about God's judgment as a cup of wrath, Jeremiah pointed out that God was bringing evil upon Jerusalem. Subsequently this cup would be given to surrounding nations. Thus he advised that they should submit themselves to the Babylonian ruler and that resistance was futile.

After the extensive exilic exodus from Jerusalem in 597 B.C., Jeremiah sent letters to the exiles who were impatiently hoping to return at an early opportunity, since they did not believe that Jerusalem would be destroyed. Jeremiah's advice was that they should settle in Babylonia, plant vineyards, and build houses because the captivity would last seventy years.

A greater restoration than the return from Babylon is promised by Jeremiah. With more forceful and explicit statements than any other prophet had made, he asserts that Israel's kingdom will be restored in the regathering of the Israelites from the ends of the earth (chaps. 30–33). At least part of this message was given when the armies of Babylon were besieging Jerusalem before its fall in 586 B.C.

When the fall of Jerusalem seemed to be inevitable even to those who had so far refused to believe God's message, Jeremiah was instructed to purchase property as a sign of future restoration. Although he had specifically predicted a return after seventy years, these chapters focus attention primarily upon the ultimate return in the final regathering of Israel. As God had watched over them in their dispersion, so He would direct them in their return.

The conditions prevailing in this restored state stand in contrast to the disintegration of the temporal kingdom. A branch of righteousness of Davidic seed shall rule, executing righteousness throughout the land. A new covenant will be established —unlike the previous one which the Israelites had broken through their disobedience. God's law will be inscribed on their hearts so that in practice they will be His people. Each individual will know God with a consciousness of sins forgiven. Gathered in Zion in a state of absolute peace, God's people will rejoice and prosper.

The core of Jeremiah's message seems to be summarized in 9:23–24. God's message is:

> Never boast if you are
> > wise—in your wisdom
> > strong—in your strength
> > rich—in your riches.
>
> If you want to boast, boast in
> > your insight and recognition that God delights to
> > > rule with kindness and love

give true decisions
exercise righteousness on the earth.

Wisdom, power and riches accrued by man are but temporary sources of security, whereas from the eternal perspective it is God who exercises love, justice, and righteousness. Consequently, the one who maintains a relationship with God is justified in boasting. Jeremiah is confident that the person who responds responsibly to God's love will not need to fear the execution of God's justice and righteousness. When the true and living God who is the King of Israel as well as the King of all nations will punish the uncircumcised, even the Israelites will be judged for their uncircumcision of the heart (9:25–10:16). Those, however, who know God properly and in obedience maintain the covenant relationship are among those who belong to and are identified with the Lord of Hosts. Conscious of the temporality of all things in this life and the ultimate judgment of God, Jeremiah was concerned that each man should have a proper knowledge of Him.

EZEKIEL—JUDGMENT AND HOPES FOR RESTORATION

Ezekiel ministered to the Israelites in exile while Jeremiah continued in Jerusalem until the city capitulated to the Babylonian conquerors in 586 B.C. Taken captive to Babylon in 597 with some ten thousand Judaean citizens, Ezekiel responded to God's call in 593 B.C. Although removed from their homeland, these fellow exiles shared the conviction of Jeremiah's audience that Jerusalem would not be destroyed. Consequently they falsely hoped to return to Jerusalem at the earliest opportunity even though Jeremiah had by letters admonished them to plan on a seventy-year captivity (Jer. 29:10).

Ezekiel's charge was simple and direct. The Israelites had failed to obey and had even scorned God's requirements of them in their covenant relationship. They had not lived as

God's holy people (5:6). They had defiled the sanctuary, even including idolatry in their religious life.

Unique in Ezekiel's message is the vivid portrayal of God's glory which represented His presence among His people. Theologically correct were those who maintained that the temple in Jerusalem was God's dwelling place even as the tabernacle had been previously since the Sinai revelation under Moses. When Solomon dedicated the temple, the people witnessed the manifestation of God's glory which filled the temple (II Chron. 7:1-3). In the vision (Ezek. 8-11), which Ezekiel shared with the elders in exile, he dramatically portrayed the departure of God's glory or presence from the temple. God abandons the temple as well as the city to utter destruction.

The reasons for this drastic judgment are clearly stated. The sanctuary of God had been defiled: elders tolerated, approved, and participated in idolatry; the women were weeping to the foreign god Tammuz in the gate of the Lord's house; and twenty-five leading men were worshiping the sun with their backs to the temple. Acknowledgment of God's presence and true worship had been replaced by blatant idolatry. Bloodshed and injustice permeated their daily lives, while love and respect for each other were conspicuously absent. God's fury and wrath are now due upon the Israelites for their evil deeds (5:12-17; 9:9-10).

The relationship between the individual and God is significantly emphasized by Ezekiel as the nation of Israel is subjected to God's wrath in the razing of the temple, the destruction of Jerusalem, and the exile of the populace. The soul that sinneth shall die (18:20) is the timely warning. The wicked will not be saved because of the presence of the righteous, nor will the righteous perish with the wicked in judgment. In God's perfect justice each individual will receive his just dues.

Mercy preceded this great outpouring of God's wrath. Repeatedly Ezekiel warned the people to repent (cf. 14:6-11), even as prophet after prophet had done in times past and as

Jeremiah was doing in Jerusalem until the actual destruction occurred. Even in the execution of divine judgment the individuals who "groan and lament over all the abominations" (9:4) that prevailed in Jerusalem were carefully marked and spared. In this way the God-fearing individuals continued to be favored with His everlasting mercy.

"Harlotry" epitomized the relationship between God and the Israelites in the message of Ezekiel (23:1–49). Samaria had been untrue to God and had courted Assyrian favor, but subsequently the people of the Northern Kingdom had been exiled to Assyria. Jerusalem, which had survived Assyrian might through God's providential care, incurred double guilt. For her idolatrous ways Jerusalem was doomed for destruction by the Babylonian kingdom.

Hope is expressed in the tender relationship of a shepherd and his sheep after the destruction of Jerusalem actually occurs (Ezek. 34). False shepherds had influenced the Israelites to deviate from their wholehearted commitment to God and had led them to national ruination, as Moses had forewarned them (Lev. 26:14–23). Now God, as the Great Shepherd, promises ultimate restoration, which is portrayed in the Davidic ideal. Ezekiel explicitly predicts that this kingdom will be restored.

Exiled to the ends of the earth for their sins, the Israelites are to be regathered. This is vividly portrayed in the vision of the valley of dry bones. Even as these bones supernaturally take on life, so the Israelites are to be gathered and restored as a nation. Challenged by a northern confederacy, they will ultimately be reestablished in their own land. The presence of God will be manifest among them as the glory of God once more fills the temple.

Repeatedly the relationship between God and the Israelites is expressed in the statement, "They shall know that I am the Lord." Although they had intellectual and theological knowledge about God based on the Mosaic revelation, Ezekiel's people did not live in accordance with a realistic awareness of what

God was like. If they ignored the warning of the prophets, continued to rebel, and failed to repent, then God's judgment executed upon Israel would bring them to the realization that God is just and righteous, punishing sin (5:13–16:13). Through these developments the Israelites would acknowledge God as they endured the consequences of having previously ignored His love and mercy.

Now Israel would also know God in His everlasting mercy. When they are regathered from exile, the Israelites as well as the heathen will realize what God is like (36:21–38). In their national revival and the establishment of the kingdom, the Israelites will in reality "know that I am the Lord."

DANIEL—THE KINGDOM PERSPECTIVE

The most detailed and extensive perspective of international developments as related to the Jewish nation came in the revelation to the prophet Daniel. Taken as a royal hostage to Babylon in 605 B.C., he rose almost immediately to a top administrative post under Nebuchadnezzar. Although he possibly was inactive under subsequent rulers, he was promised third place in the Babylonian kingdom on the eve of Babylon's conquest by Cyrus. In the Medo-Persian kingdom, Daniel once again was given a very responsible position.

Daniel was keenly conscious of his personal relationship with God. His wholehearted commitment to Him is reflected in his concern not to defile himself in the idolatrous environs of the royal court in Babylon (chap. 1). This reverence or fear of God is also expressed by Daniel in his courteous attitude toward his superiors during his captivity. Completely divorced from the legalistic or ritualistic observance of the law associated with the temple in Jerusalem, Daniel exemplified a concern for making the heart of the Mosaic revelation—a wholehearted love for God—a practical reality in his daily pattern of living.

Throughout his life Daniel apparently maintained this vital

relationship with God. In the crucial experience (chap. 2) when he faced execution, Daniel, together with the companions, prayed for "mercy of the God of Heaven." Subsequently through a divine revelation he was enabled to relate to King Nebuchadnezzar his dream and its interpretation.

This king of Babylon recognized Daniel as a God-fearing person. Daniel had his first opportunity to share his knowledge of God as he reported the dream and its interpretation, indicating that ultimately the God of heaven would establish a kingdom without end. Subsequently when Nebuchadnezzar had another dream he turned to Daniel, acknowledging that Daniel had the spirit of the holy God (chap. 4). Years later when Belshazzar was faced with the mysterious handwriting on the banquet-room wall, Daniel once again was singled out as a man who had a vital relationship with God (chap. 5). In response to the king's request, he interpreted the sobering announcement of God's judgment.

In the Medo-Persian era, when Daniel had again risen to a top-level administrative position, the character of Daniel emerges once more as that of a God-fearing person. It is apparent that Daniel in his daily life reflected a consciousness of God. After a thorough investigation his political critics found nothing questionable about his ethics and practices in his administrative responsibilities or in his relationship with his fellow men. His standard of morality and pattern of daily living were beyond criticism. No charges of injustice or bribery could be directed against him. The crucial point in which they temporarily succeeded in indicting him was the matter of his wholehearted devotion to God.

Daniel's devotion to God is clearly delineated in 6:10. Prayer seemed to be part of his daily pattern of living as he expressed his thanksgiving to God in an attitude of true worship. The fact that he faced Jerusalem suggests that he had a concern for the future of the Jewish nation. Even though he had personally prospered he had not permitted the endowment of political power and prestige to diminish his love for God and the promises made to his people Israel. It was the reading of Jeremiah that prompted him to intercede earnestly in intercessory prayer for the restoration of Israel (9:1ff.).

To the man Daniel came the unique revelation about the future developments from the international perspective. That a series of kingdoms would rise and fall is repeatedly indicated through Nebuchadnezzar's dream and subsequent divine revelations to Daniel. Although these provide a general outline of future developments which have been subject to varied interpretations, certain aspects seem to emerge explicitly in the scriptural text and context.

Nebuchadnezzar is identified as the head of gold, indicating that Babylonia is the first of successive kingdoms (2:37). Daniel, in response to his inquiry and concern, is divinely informed that Medo-Persia and Greece will follow as great powers of international might (8:20–26). The latter will be divided into four parts. A God-defiant king will inflict persecution on the saints but his power will be broken by nonhuman might.

Another aspect of this kingdom series is the perspective of an ultimate kingdom that will endure forever (2:44–45; 7:13–14, 18, 21–27). This kingdom will be established through supernatural intervention, since the ruler is identified as the God of heaven or Ancient of Days. Associated with him in this reign are the "saints" or "people of the saints of the Most High." In all likelihood these saints are later identified to Daniel as "your people" (in 9:24 and 12:1–4), referring to the remnant of Israel who are delivered out of great trouble and joined by those who are resurrected to everlasting life.

The total period allotted to Daniel's people is seventy weeks (9:24), usually translated as "seventy weeks of years" making a total of 490 years. These weeks are divided into three periods, consisting of seven weeks or forty-nine years, sixty-two weeks or 434 years, and one week or seven years. The starting point of this seventy-week period is the command to rebuild Jerusalem. The first two periods terminate with the appearance of the Messiah who was subsequently "cut off." The final one week, or seven years, seems to be a subsequent period interrupted in the middle by the termination of sacrifice and offering. The fact that the total period for Israel is seventy weeks suggests that this last seven-year period immediately precedes the consummation of all things or the beginning of the everlasting kingdom which was the climax for Daniel's people, as indicated previously.

Unlike Isaiah, the prophetic perspective of Daniel does not include the mission of the suffering servant through whom salvation is extended to the Gentiles. Daniel, primarily viewing developments from the pinnacle of powerful kingdoms, sees through divine revelation the final restoration prospects for his people Israel. Even though his people will be subjected to suffering intensively under God-defiant rulers, these kingdoms will finally be terminated as the everlasting kingdom emerges. Daniel is personally assured that he will stand in his lot at the end of the days.

HAGGAI—TEMPLE REBUILDING

Nearly two decades had passed since the exiles returned from Babylon to Jerusalem when Haggai delivered his prophetic messages. Although they had immediately resumed sacrifice and festal activities (Ezra 1–3), their enemies successfully kept them from rebuilding the temple. Consequently they had become absorbed in building fine houses for their own comfort.

Haggai, as a prophet speaking for God, was primarily concerned about their relationship with God. They had become so engrossed with selfish, materialistic interests of building beautiful homes that they lacked motivation to rebuilt the Lord's house (1:7). The sacrifices and services they rendered were not pleasing to God because the people themselves were not genuinely devoted to God (2:10–14). Service and sacrifice offered by the people who lacked a wholehearted love for God were not favorable to obtaining God's blessing. Haggai assured them of God's favor and prosperity if they turned their attention to the rebuilding of the temple.

ZECHARIAH—ISRAEL IN GOD'S PERSPECTIVE

Explicitly Zechariah points out in his introductory message that the temple was reduced to ruins because the Israelites' forefathers had not listened to the warnings of the prophets. Their rebellious attitude and lack of reverence, respect, and wholehearted love toward God had precipitated this terrible judgment in the destruction of Jerusalem. Maintaining a right relationship with God—this is the lesson the returning exiles ought to learn from history, asserts Zechariah. They ought to repent and not act as their fathers did (1:1–6).

What about future prospects? Since the previous temple was destroyed, what will happen to this one if they succeed in rebuilding it? What about Israel's guilt? What about the long-range hopes of restoration of the kingdom of Israel? In symbolic language Zechariah answers these questions in his second message, based on a series of visions (1:7–6:14). Although much of this passage is obscure, the main ideas are more readily apparent.

Presently God, the Lord of Hosts, is returning with mercy and compassion to Jerusalem. The temple will be rebuilt. Prosperity and comfort are in store for Jerusalem and Judah. The world powers that scattered the Israelites will be terminated (1:7–21).

A vast expansion of Jerusalem, extending the population far beyond the city walls, is assured. Even in Nehemiah's time, about seventy years later, such vast areas within the walled boundary of Jerusalem were unoccupied that a conscription was necessary to bring residents from surrounding towns to establish homes in the city so that the wall would be properly guarded (Neh. 11:1–2). Such a population expansion envisioned by Zechariah has not yet been realized even today, since with it the Lord Himself will be the glory of the Holy City of Jerusalem and will provide a wall of fire for protection.

Atonement for Israel's sin was assured in the divine provision qualifying Joshua to sacrifice so that Israel could be restored to a right relationship with God. With this came the promise of God's future provision in His Servant, the branch through whom the sin of Israel would be removed in a single day. After this, absolute peace and prosperity will prevail so that everyone with his neighbor will dwell in security (3:1–10).

The Lord's continual everlasting watchfulness over Israel is vividly portrayed in the automatic unending supply of oil for the golden seven-lipped lampstand furnished by two olive trees. The latter represented the two anointed ones who assist the Lord whose eyes see everywhere throughout the whole earth (4:1–14).

Although the flying scroll explicitly stated Israel's guilt in transgression, comfort came in the realization that the iniquity of Israel was transported to the land of Shinar, or Babylon (5:1–11). With the chariots patrolling the whole earth and the crowning of Joshua, the audience of Zechariah is again offered assurance that the Lord of Hosts is in control. Through their obedience to Him they can proceed in confidence as they rebuild the temple of God.

When the question of the traditional fast was raised two years later, Zechariah pointedly elaborated on the basic problem of Israel's relationship with God. Fasting for the sake of fasting was futile. Observance of feasts and perfunctory performances of rituals were useless in an attitude of self-interest instead of wholehearted devotion to God. Wrath and divine judgment had come to their forefathers because they failed in demonstrating justice and love toward their fellow men, even ignoring the warnings given through the prophets (7:1–14).

By contrast to the destroyed city which in his day was partially occupied, Zechariah assures this small discouraged remnant of the ultimate peace and prosperity awaiting Jerusalem (8:1–23). Israelites will be gathered from the east and from the west. Jerusalem will be known as the "faithful city and the mountain of the Lord of hosts, the holy mountain." So evident will the divine blessing be in Jerusalem that nations and individuals will curry the favor of the Jews to seek the Lord of Hosts. With these words Zechariah encouraged the generation in which he was living to continue diligently in the building of the temple that had previously been razed in judgment because of the sins of their forefathers.

In typical prophetic language, Zechariah projects in the final part of his book the conditions related to the establishment of the ultimate kingdom. Although numerous aspects of these unfolding plans seem ambiguous, certain features emerge as various parts of this message are integrated.

Jerusalem is crucially important in these final developments. Nations who become involved with the city of Jerusalem will find it to be a burdensome stone or a cup of poison to their own destruction or ruination (12:2–3). The Lord will protect Jerusalem, seeking to destroy all nations that declare war against it (12:8). The residents of Jerusalem will be endued with a spirit of compassion and prayer so that they will recognize "Him whom they have pierced" (12:10). Security and holiness will prevail throughout the city of Jerusalem (14:11, 20–21). From the city of Jerusalem will issue streams of living water (14:8).

Israel will be regathered from distant lands even as a shepherd gathers his sheep (10:8–12). Non-Israelites who intermarry with them will worship the true God instead of the Israelites' turning to the idols of surrounding nations (9:1–8). Israel will be refined by fire, suffering in the conflict and losing about two-thirds of its population. The remnant, or remaining third, will genuinely acknowledge God. Cleansing from iniquity will be provided for Israel so that idolatry, false prophets, and deceivers will be totally removed from the land (13:1–9). They will acknowledge and rejoice in the Lord as their God (13:1–9).

Other nations will challenge Israel's regathering and will mobilize against Jerusalem (14:1–6), but God will intervene for Israel. Enemies will be blinded (12:4) and panic-stricken, so that their wealth will be confiscated (14:12–15). Rain will be withheld from all who refuse to worship God.

God's covenant with Israel has not been forgotten. Israel's deliverance comes because of God's covenant (9:11–17). The restoration of Israel was a manifestation of God's compassion and love extended to them (10:6).

The King of Zion is portrayed as one who is victorious and triumphant yet humble and riding upon an ass (9:9). Although this aspect of his humble appearance was realized in the triumphal entry of Jesus into Jerusalem, the establishment of a worldwide dominion when He will speak peace to the nations awaits fulfillment (9:10). As King, the Lord will appear on the Mount of Olives, dividing it from east to west to fight against the nations gathered against Jerusalem (14:1–8). In a continuous day, or unending period, the Lord will become King over all the earth. The survivors of all nations will worship the Lord of Hosts and participate in the sacred festivities. In this manner the ultimate kingdom will be established with the Israelites enjoying absolute peace and prosperity in their own land.

MALACHI—A GOD-SENT MESSENGER PROMISED

In a concise and pointed message Malachi speaks directly to the issue of man's relationship with God. He indicts his audience for not responding to God's love and for mistreating their fellow men. For ignoring this law of love they will be judged by God. Individual accountability is certain, since God will divide the righteous and the wicked for reward and punishment. Before that day of ultimate judgment God will send His Messenger, providing another opportunity to repent.

"I have loved you," says Malachi, speaking for God. This

points back to the heart of the covenant relationship established under Moses. God is the Great King (1:14). The day is coming when He will be greatly revered by all Gentiles and yet the Israelites now fail to revere and honor Him. Their lives reflected failure on their part to respond with love, reverence, and honor in their attitude toward God.

The priests or religious leaders bear the greatest guilt. They offered polluted sacrifices and were guilty of advising people that they could bring lame animals for sacrifice when they knew that God required the very best. At the same time they recited a prayer for God's mercy. How could they expect God to favor them when such hypocrisy prevailed? A father would not tolerate such treatment by his son, nor a master by his servant. How did they dare to treat God in this way? Hardly a priest could be found who would have the courage to act in accordance with God's instructions and refuse such sacrifices because they were dishonoring to God.

In the future God's name will be revered among the Gentile nations continually. The time is coming when they will offer sweet incense and bring pure, acceptable offerings genuinely honoring to God. At present the Israelites who are God's covenant people dare to bring sick animals as offerings when they appear before Him in worship. They would not think of treating their governor with such a lack of respect. They would not dare to ignore his requirements or desires in their concern to serve him. Consequently it is high time that God's people examine their relationship with God their King.

The purpose of God's covenant is clearly stated—to give life and peace (2:5-9). Moses had already asserted this when he expounded the terms of God's covenant to the generation that was about to enter and occupy Canaan (Deut. 31:1-13). The religious leaders were responsible to teach the people fear and respect for God by carefully observing what God required of them—a wholehearted love for God—in response to his love for them. Genuine love in daily life would involve a careful consideration of what God expected in sacrifice and offerings. Religious leaders who heeded the divine instructions lived a good and righteous life, and by precept and example caused others to do the same thing. It is the priest who is responsible for informing the layman what the Lord of Hosts has prescribed in the law. Unfortunately the priests were showing partiality in interpreting and administering the law—for this they would be judged.

The basic problem was not one of legalism. Their attitude toward God was not right (2:10–17). Their theology was correct or orthodox in recognizing that God had created each one of them. However, they seemed to blame God for the fact that they were mistreating each other, failing to show love for one another. While partial in their teaching of the law, profaning the sanctuary, accepting inferior offerings, weeping and groaning or complaining at the altar because their offerings were not accepted, the leaders assure the people that God delights in their pattern of living and naïvely ask, "Where is the God of justice or judgment?"

A God-sent Messenger is promised (3:1–5). This one will come for a twofold purpose. He will refine and purify people so that acceptable offerings will once again be offered. He will also come to judge. Justice will be meted out to those who have mistreated their fellow men. God's mercy will be terminated for those who, instead of loving their neighbors, trick the innocent, commit adultery, lie, cheat the wage-earner, take advantage of widows and orphans, turn aside the foreigners or strangers, and fail to revere or fear God. All these evil deeds, concerning which there was ample warning in the Mosaic revelation, cannot be overlooked by God their King.

Having delineated their failure to practice love toward one another, Malachi directs or reverts his message again to the basic problem: failure to love and revere God (3:6–15). God's day of judgment is certain, but this day is not dated. Presently God's mercy is still extended, providing opportunity for them to repent and confess their sin. Their failure to acknowledge their sin toward God brings into consideration another indictment that can be definitely identified: they have robbed God by not giving Him a tenth of their income. Pride and arrogance, however, are at the basis of their failure to acknowledge God.

The gospel of love is definitely applied as Malachi speaks of the final judgment. The basis for divine judgment of men is vividly delineated. The Great King who extended His love and mercy in His covenant treaty with Israel will execute judgment for each individual on the basis of his personal response to God's love (3:16–4:6). Those who love God, respecting and revering Him so that they have applied the instructions divinely revealed through Moses concerning their relationship to their fellow men, will be spared by God in the day of judgment. They have their names recorded in God's book of remembrance. Upon them God's mercy will continue without end.

The arrogant, the proud, those who have ignored or failed to respond to God's love for them so that they have spurned God's instructions concerning neighborly love, those who have considered it foolish to worship God, or have been unwilling to confess their sin—these face the day of judgment before the Great King. For them the day of judgment is coming like a burning furnace.

Malachi, like Moses and the other prophets, points to the basic responsibility of man to love and revere God. A genuine love for God should also be reflected in this relationship with his fellow men. For these there is the promise of God's everlasting mercy. Likewise Malachi agrees with the prophets before him that those who don't love and respect God await the day of God's judgment and curse.

Malachi's message concludes with hope for his generation. Before that dreadful day of judgment God is sending His Messenger to turn people Godward. Mercy precedes God's final judgment. God's love still prevails.

X

THE GOSPEL
FOR THIS AGE

Jesus came as the fullness of the manifestation of God's love to the human race. Throughout Old Testament times the divine promises were given and reaffirmed from generation to generation pointing forward to the revelation of a God-man in whom was vested the essence of salvation as well as the promise of an everlasting kingdom.

THE PROMISE OF REDEMPTION

The initial promise in the crucial crisis after Adam and Eve had broken their fellowship with God was the divine assurance of ultimate victory through their posterity (Gen. 3:15). In a subsequent judgment upon sinful man, God-fearing Noah and his family were the recipients of God's mercy and preservation. Among Noah's wayward posterity it was Abraham who responded to divine revelation in active faith to leave his idolatrous family and migrate to Canaan. God's promise to him was that through his posterity all the nations of the world would be blessed (Gen. 12:1–3). In the unfolding of the future reality of this divine commitment to Abraham the land of Canaan was assured as a possession to his descendants.

In Egypt the divine promise issued into a national perspective. God's involvement of Moses and the divine acts in which the Israelites were miraculously released from Egyptian enslavement provided the basis for the establishment of Israel as God's chosen nation. En route to Canaan to occupy the land promised previously to Abraham the Israelites were the recipients of God's greatest revelation in Old Testament times. Having experienced God's love in redemptive power the Israelites were to live as His holy people exclusively devoted to God. Moses epitomizes the two governing principles in two brief statements:

> Love God with all your heart.
> Love your neighbor as yourself.

Israel was chosen to be God's servant in order to bring salvation to all the nations of the world. When the Moabite king Balak attempted to have the Israelites cursed, Balaam blessed the nation of Israel with the promise of a superior kingdom (Num. 22–24). To David in the era of Israel's most extensive kingdom achievement came the divine promise that his throne would endure forever.

As the national hopes for Israel declined to the point of judgment and doom in the centuries after the reigns of David and Solomon (931–586 B.C.), the promise of this everlasting ultimate kingdom was renewed and enlarged. When godless Ahaz was ruling on the Davidic throne in Jerusalem the prophet Isaiah gave assurance of the birth of a son to be called Immanuel (7:14) and identified as Mighty God (9:6). For the apostate kingdom Isaiah announced the impending doom of Jerusalem (chaps. 1–5) but gave assurance of a restoration in which Zion would be the capital of a universal kingdom permeated by absolute peace (2:1–4; 9:7; 11:1–9; 35:1–10). This kingdom will have a ruler who executes righteousness, justice, and equity. Unlike contemporary kings on the Davidic throne, this God-placed ruler in Zion will not disappoint those who place their confidence and trust in him (28:16).

In the wake of Isaiah's prediction of Babylonian captivity (39:1–8) the promise of a threefold restoration for Israel is delineated in chapters 40 through 66. Israel as God's servant (41:8) was punitively suffering in exile but would be released through Cyrus divinely identified as "My shepherd" and "His anointed" (44:28–45:1).

Inasmuch as God's servant Israel failed in her mission to "bring justice to the nations" and to be a "light to the nations" (42:1, 6) God is sending His Servant to restore Israel and to provide a light to the nations so that salvation may be extended to earth's farthest bounds (49:1–6). The mission of this Servant culminates in his vicarious death being portrayed in chapter 53 as the "Righteous One" dying for the sins of others. The divine invitation—and assurance of God's love as it had been promised to David—offers life, pardon and forgiveness of sin, and restoration to all people universally (55:1–56:8). The people who respond to this invitation—those who "love the name of the Lord"—are identified as God's servants (54:17; 56:6; 65:8ff.). God's house is not limited to the Israelites but will be a "house of prayer for all nations" (56:8).

The assurance for the restoration of Jerusalem is vested in the promise of a redeemer coming to Zion (59:16–62:12). Jerusalem will again be restored (62:7) and known as "the Zion of the Holy One of Israel" (60:14). Kings and nations will bring their wealth in adoration and worship in this ultimate kingdom so that "Jerusalem will be the praise of all the earth."

The initial promise to man provided the basic element of ultimate victory over the enemy through a descendant of Eve (Gen. 3:15). As God's promise was enlarged and related to the contemporary developments as the prophets communicated God's message, it became clear that restoration for man would be vested in an individual who was Godlike or who had divine qualities when born as a babe into the human race. This was most comprehensively delineated by Isaiah and complemented by other prophets. On the basis of these promises the Israelites

expected salvation for them as a nation in the coming of the
Messiah.

THE GOD-MAN RECOGNIZED

When Jesus was born he was identified with the promises
given throughout Old Testament times. In the divine disclosure
by the angel Gabriel (Luke 1:26–38) to the virgin Mary, Jesus
was called "the Son of the Most High" to whom the Lord God
will give "the throne of His father David" and "He will reign
over the house of Jacob forever; and His kingdom will have no
end." Mary is assured that her son "shall be called the Son of
God." After Jesus is born in the city of David he is designated
as a "Savior who is Christ the Lord" (Luke 2:11). Zechariah
recognized the divine visitation as the means of bringing salvation through the house of David (Luke 1:68). Simeon equated
Jesus with the servant who provided

> a light to enlighten the Gentiles and
> the glory of God's people Israel (Luke 2:32).

Andrew introduced his brother Peter to Jesus with the excit-
ing recognition "We have found the Messiah" (John 1:41). Philip
identified Jesus as the person about whom Moses and the prophets had written (John 1:45). Nathaniel met Jesus with the accla-
mation, "Rabbi, you are the Son of God; you are the King of
Israel" (John 1:49). When the disciples report on the identification of Jesus by the populace it was Peter who declared his
conviction, addressing Jesus directly, "You are the Christ [Mes-
siah], the son of the living God" (Matt. 16:16).

After the death and resurrection of Jesus, the disciples boldly
asserted before the multitudes assembled in Jerusalem that
Jesus was the individual spoken of by Moses and the prophets.
Peter identified Jesus as the prophet promised by Moses and
other prophets (Acts 3:18–26). Stephen delineated before the
Sanhedrin, the most learned body of Israelites assembled in

Jerusalem, the divine revelation throughout Old Testament times beginning with Abraham. Boldly he asserted that "the Righteous One" (cf. Isa. 53:11) who had been announced by the prophets is Jesus whom they had betrayed (Acts 7). Philip, as he conversed with the Ethiopian eunuch, identified Jesus with the suffering individual portrayed in Isaiah 53 (Acts 8:26–40).

Paul, the greatest of the apostles, expounded the Old Testament, explicitly asserting that the promises made to the Israelites beginning with Abraham were fulfilled in the person of Jesus Christ (Acts 13:16–41). Again in a subsequent mission Paul addressed a synagogue audience and "reasoned with them from the Scriptures" boldly declaring that "This Jesus I am proclaiming to you is the Christ" (Messiah) about whom the prophets wrote (Acts 17:2–3). On the occasion of defending his life before King Agrippa, Paul firmly pointed out that Jesus Christ through His death and resurrection fulfilled what was predicted by Moses and the prophets (Acts 26:1–32).

In this manner Jesus was recognized as the God-man in whom the divine promises, imparted to the human race especially through Abraham and his heirs, found fulfillment. The author of the letter to the Hebrews concurs with this when he observes, "In the past God spoke to our forefathers through the prophets at many times and in various ways, but in these last days he has spoken to us by His Son. . . ."

SELF-DISCLOSURE BY JESUS

Jesus Himself emerged as a teacher who unlike any prophets before Him claimed that He was the God-man. In simple language He asserted that He was the water and bread of life, the light of the world, the way, the truth, the resurrection and the life. Speaking with authority He positively affirmed that He was the manifestation of God Himself (John 14:7–12). Repeatedly in His teaching ministry He pointed to the Old Testament Scriptures, declaring dogmatically that He fulfilled what was written concerning Him. Specifically He identified Himself with the prediction in Isaiah 61:1 after reading this passage publicly in a synagogue in Nazareth (Luke 4:16–21).

Christ's claim to divinity became an issue so disturbing to the religious leaders of His day that after numerous crises it led to His trial and death. When, at the time of Christ's triumphal entry into Jerusalem, the multitude addressed to Jesus the prayer in Psalm 118:25, which was directed to God by the psalmist, the religious leaders were enraged. Unable to control the multitude, the Pharisees appealed to Jesus to rebuke His disciples and the children. By this desperate appeal the critics directly confronted Jesus with His claim to be equal with God and on that basis accepting prayer and praise which the psalmist had addressed to God. No prophet before, or apostle later, ever allowed himself such acclaim. Instead of pacifying His critics, Jesus Christ rebuked them with the words of the psalmist, "Out of the mouth of babes and sucklings thou hast perfected praise" (Matt. 21:1–17; Luke 19:28–40).

Unlike the prophets before Him, Jesus accepted worship. When He identified Himself as the Son of God to the blind man whose sight had been restored, Jesus accepted his response in faith and worship (John 9:35–38). Other individuals who worshiped Jesus were the leper (Matt. 8:2), a certain ruler (Matt. 9:18), and the woman of Canaan (Matt. 15:25).

The claims of Jesus were temporarily silenced with the crucifixion. The resurrection, however, uniquely confirmed His disclosure that He was the Son of God.

JESUS AND THE LAW

Jesus came to fulfill the law and the prophets—not to abolish them. The crucial passage (Matt. 5:17–20) deserves careful consideration as it relates to the Scriptures, the cultural and religious context, and the mission of Jesus.

Frequently this statement by Jesus has been interpreted as

referring only to the law of Moses. Jesus, however, specifically says the law and the prophets—a descriptive reference used repeatedly in the New Testament to identify that body of literature which the Jews regarded as inspired and which was in the Christian era and is today commonly called the Old Testament.

Although the word "law" in Matthew 5:18 could be interpreted in a restricted sense, it is likewise possible that Jesus here referred to the entire Old Testament. Such seems to be the case in John 10:34 where Jesus quotes from Psalm 82 and reminds His listeners that this is written in their law. This may also be the meaning of the term "law" in Luke 16:17 where it could represent the entire Jewish canon.

The Scriptures were regarded by the Jews as the expression of God's will. They represented the written revelation of what God wanted His people to know as He had revealed it through Moses and the prophets. The divine revelation through Moses established Israel as a nation, as recorded in Exodus through Deuteronomy. The essential background and introduction is given in Genesis where God's relationship to the entire human race and the patriarchs is unfolded. The historical account and the messages of the prophets were considered an essential part of the Scriptures as they provided supplementary information to the Mosaic revelation as it was given through the prophets. In "Moses and all the prophets" much had been written concerning the promises of God and the restoration of the kingdom.

How did the Jews observe the law? What was the established pattern of religion as taught and practiced in Judaism at the time Jesus lived in Palestine?

In the post-exilic era an intensive concern for keeping the law was a distinctive mark of Israel's religion. Throughout the centuries of political tensions, as Persian domination gave way to Greek and Roman supremacy, bringing changing cultures and fortunes to bear upon the Jews, the pattern of living prescribed for God's holy people became the focal point of interest.

As the study of the law increased, disciples gathered around teachers such as Ben Sira (Ecclus. 38:24–34; 51:23). Very likely he belonged to the professional scribes and may have conducted an academy in Jerusalem where he lectured to youth on ethical and religious subjects. In the course of time many of the commands in the law were given detailed definitions and interpretations (Jubilee 50:1–13). By way of example, the Sabbath law could be suspended for defense purposes (Macc. 2:29–41). In this way a hedge was built around the law (P. Aboth 1:1) as adjustment was made to the changing situations in varied circumstances.

For many generations these interpretations were transmitted orally and became known as oral laws. Sects such as the Sadducees and the Pharisees developed, reflecting varied views of interpretation. The latter advocated minute observance of the law and made the oral law obligatory, while the former accepted only the Torah. By about A.D. 200 these oral laws were codified in the Mishnah and later completed in the Talmud. Although the list of 613 laws was completed in medieval times by Maimonides, it is generally held that the broad outlines of these were part of the oral tradition of first-century Judaism.

Regardless of sect, however, basic in the religion of the Jews was the concern to fulfill the requirements of the written law. The sum of all righteousness was to keep the law. Consequently Judaism was constantly facing the danger of legalism or of becoming a religion in which a man's works determined his status before God. This externalizing of righteousness was seemingly never checked in Judaism in subsequent centuries.

The moral and ethical teachings in the synagogue during the middle forty years of the first century of the Christian era are best known to us through the Gospels. Jesus in His ministry of teaching and healing constantly mingled with all classes of society from publicans and sinners to the most righteous among the religious leaders. Numerous dialogues between Jesus and Pharisees, Sadducees, and scribes provide insight into the religious climate during that generation. Added to these are the discourses of Jesus and that which He taught by way of example.

The extensive legalistic externalism reflected in the Mishnah and later in the Talmud should not be regarded as the norm for Judaism in the days of Jesus. Pharisaic piety is definitely portrayed as being primarily formalistic or external. John the Baptist referred to the Pharisees, as well as the Sadducees and the multitude (Matt. 3:7ff.; Luke 3:7ff.), as a "generation of vipers" as far as their relationship with God was concerned. Jesus disclosed their hearts as being evil while they pretended to exhibit good outward deeds (Matt. 12:33–37). In His teaching, Jesus described the external righteousness of the Pharisees but indicated that a higher standard was necessary to enter the kingdom (Matt. 5:20–6:18; Luke 11:42). Jesus' incisive observation was that they honored God with their lips but their hearts were far removed from Him (Matt. 7:1–20; Mark 7:1–23). In His indictment of the scribes and the Pharisees, He identified them as hypocrites.

Josephus likewise points to external piety when he reports that a certain Pharisee named Ananias observed the religious fast for the purpose of achieving his political goals. Furthermore, sacred festivals were often observed by Jewish leaders for political advantages. Seditions were frequently initiated during these religious observances. According to Josephus, such formalistic piety was an accepted standard for many Jews.

The fact that external piety so extensively permeated Judaism during the time of Jesus should not obscure the fact that there were individuals who reflected true genuine religion. Mechanical conformity to the law was never the aim or objective of the most devout teachers. Hillel and some of the other Jewish teachers of that era are quoted in the early Jewish writings as emphasizing the fact that the external rites and actions in themselves are not meritorious and that a good heart is the source of all good. Significant is the fact that in the *Shema*, which was recited daily by the Jews in this early period, the matter of obedience came third in order after a confession or affirmation of the unity of God and man. This order was also followed in the *Shemoneh Esreh* (the "Eighteen Benedictions") and the 613 commandments. The service of man came in order after the acknowledgment of God and of a wholehearted love for Him. Through these the Talmudic emphasis of the love of God as the proper motivation for living the religious life seems to reflect the concern of the best teachers in Jewish history even before A.D. 70 when the temple was destroyed.

The Gospels as well as Josephus bear witness that there were some religious leaders who had the Mosaic perspective of what was important in man's relationship with God. Jesus spoke favorably of one scribe who recognized that love for God and man had priority over ritualism and service (Mark 12:28–34). Consider also Nicodemus (John 3:1; 19:39), Joseph of Arimathea (Mark 15:43), and other Pharisees who were favorably disposed toward Jesus and His teaching (Luke 13:31; 14:1). Josephus reports that Alexander Jannaeus considered most of the Pharisees scoundrels but did recognize a Godly element among them.

Although the religious climate into which Jesus came seemed to be predominantly legalistic, there were those who had a sense of true righteousness. The concept of a genuine mutual love relationship between man and God and the consideration for one's fellow men was still preserved by some of the leading teachers and by a minority of God-fearing people even among the Pharisees.

Without question Jesus penetrated the multitude of conflicting interpretations of the law which were so well known to that generation, and spoke with authority concerning the true meaning and interpretation of God's will. It was necessary to cut through the casuistry and legalism associated with the observance of the law. This, however, should not obscure the broader scope of Jesus' statement in asserting that He came to fulfill the law and the prophets.

How did Jesus approach the problem of fulfilling the requirements of the law and the prophets which Judaism considered the basis to faith and practice? In a dialogue with His severest critics when questioned by a lawyer of the Pharisees, Jesus made several observations which are crucial to this issue. Without the dispute of His critics, Jesus pointed to the two requirements which represented the heart of the law, namely, genuine love for God and for one's neighbor. Jesus added the significant observation that everything in the law and the prophets depended upon these requirements (Matt. 22:34–40). To the scribe who recognized these as more important than the external conformity to the law in bringing offerings and sacrifices, Jesus gave the assuring words, "You are not far from the kingdom of God" (Mark 12:28–34). The lawyer, who may have participated in this same discussion and posed the question, "What shall I do to inherit eternal life?" observed that the essential requirements of the law were to love God and to love one's neighbor as oneself. Concurring with the lawyer, Jesus assured him of eternal life (Luke 10:25–28).

There is no indication that Jesus held that the legalistic observance of the Mosaic law assured an individual of eternal life and righteousness before God. Under crucial cross examination Jesus and the contemporary religious leaders agreed that the law primarily pointed to a right relationship with God and man rather than to the legalistic observance of its details. This interpretation was confirmed by subsequent prophets and finally by Jesus Himself.

Cutting through the prevailing fabric of religious externalism, Jesus through precept and example projected a proper perspective toward that which had been revealed in the law and the prophets. Those who adhered to legalism or an outward standard of observing the law without a right relationship with God were severely denounced by Jesus. At the same time, He did not abrogate practical righteousness but asserted that those who would enter the kingdom of heaven must have a righteousness that exceeds that of the scribes and the Pharisees (Matt.

5:20; cf. also Luke 11:42). In His teaching, Jesus gave new commandments and indicated that conformity to His teaching would be genuine proof of a wholehearted love toward God. Amid the confusion of so many interpretations orally known to that generation, He authoritatively pointed out what was correct. Sensitive to the casuistry and externalism exhibited in keeping the law, Jesus pointed to its true meaning as given to Israel through Moses.

JESUS AND THE GOSPEL OF MOSES

Jesus endorsed the gospel of Moses—love God wholeheartedly and your fellow man as yourself. The basic requirements of an exclusive commitment to God and a manifestation of love to one's neighbor were as vital to a God-fearing person in New Testament times as they were when Moses stated them to the Israelites as matters of life and death before they entered the land promised to them as their possession. Love for God and neighbor, said Jesus to the scribe, is essential for man to obtain eternal life.

Jesus Christ in His incarnation represented the unique manifestation of God's love to man. Even though love and mercy were continually extended to all mankind by God in sending rain and sunshine upon the just and the unjust (Matt. 5:45), it was God's gift in sending His only Son that revealed His love for the human race (John 3:16; 17:23). The apostle Paul recognized Jesus as the expression of God's love for man (Rom. 5:8; cf. also I John 4:9).

Unfolding God's love for the human race, Jesus Christ through His life, teaching, death, and resurrection demonstrated and fulfilled that perfect commitment of love to God and fellow men in which the Israelites had failed. God had bestowed His love upon Israel (Deut. 10:12–22) with the intent that they should extend this love to their neighbors. As God's servant, Israel had failed in this mission so that God sent His only Son as the "righteous servant" to fulfill the divine plan to reach all mankind. In this manner Jesus fulfilled the mission of God's servant as delineated in Isaiah 41:8–53:12.

Throughout His life Jesus exemplified a wholehearted love and devotion to God. To Mary His mother, who found Him in the temple, Jesus replied that His foremost concern was to be in His Father's house (Luke 2:49). Frequently He withdrew from the multitude and even from His disciples in order to pray and commune with God (Matt. 14:23; Mark 1:35; Luke 5:16). To His disciples, Jesus frankly stated that doing God's will was more important to Him than food for His body (John 4:34). When wrestling with suffering and death in Gethsemane, Jesus agonized in prayer, saying, "Not my will but thine" as He communed with God (Matt. 26:36–46; Mark 14:32–43; Luke 22: 39–46). Near the end of His earthly ministry, Jesus affirmed that He had kept His Father's commandments (John 15:10).

Jesus came for the express purpose of ministering to others. He taught that love and mercy should be extended not only to those who reciprocate but to the enemy as well (Matt. 5:39–48; Luke 6:27–36; cf. also Rom. 12:20). This Godlike trait of manifesting love and mercy to the ungrateful and selfish should be characteristic of those who were sons of God. Even as Moses admonished the Israelites to love the stranger because they had been loved by God when they were strangers in Egypt (Deut. 10:19–22), so Jesus points out that those who have been recipients of God's mercy should be merciful even as God is merciful. To the lawyer who in self-justification asked, "And who is my neighbor?" Jesus gave the example of the Samaritan who out of a heart of compassion rendered social service where it was needed (Luke 10:29–37).

While Jesus lived within the framework of the written law, or Torah, He disregarded the Pharisaic principle of separation in associating with and accepting the hospitality of publicans and sinners, running the risk of ceremonial defilement (Mark 2:16; Luke 15:2; 19:7). Although severely criticized, Jesus ministered to Zaccheus, to the Samaritans, to the sinful woman who anointed Him, and to others. By allowing His disciples to pluck grain and by performing acts of healing on the Sabbath, He ignored and defied the Pharisaic restrictions and taught that the Sabbath was made for man and not man for the Sabbath (Mark 2:15–3:6). In this manner Jesus very definitely emphasized the priority of the two basic requirements of the Scriptures over the legalism that represented the outward adornment of the religious life in that generation.

Incisive and direct is Jesus' analysis of their religion when scribes and Pharisees of Jerusalem raise the issue of the disciples transgressing the traditions of the elders (Matt. 15:1–21). He boldly points out that through their traditions they have nullified the basic commandment of God. True religion begins in the heart and is not primarily judged by the outward appearance. By quoting Isaiah 29:13, Jesus identifies the heart as being far from God. When the heart, which should be the source of wholehearted love for God, is the seat of evil and defilement, then the external rites and observances fade into insignificance. Worship of God is hypocritical when human commands are taught as doctrine. In this critical evaluation Jesus taught the true meaning of God's written revelation, negating the religious framework of legalism projected through their traditions.

The legalism that Jesus encountered did not originate with Moses but had developed in Judaism during the centuries preceding the birth of Jesus. In his final appeal to the Israelites Moses admonished and challenged his generation to choose the way of life by loving God (Deut. 30:11–20).

Jesus went beyond the requirements of the law in deliberately laying down His life (John 10:7–18). This sacrifice was the fulfillment of God's particular command to Him. In this act Jesus demonstrated the "greater love" which was unprecedented in the religion of Israel (John 15:13). Through His voluntary death He exemplified His wholehearted commitment to God in obeying His commandments, thereby manifesting God's love in its fullness to man.

THE GOSPEL OF JESUS CHRIST

Jesus, having come as the essence of divine revelation, was the manifestation of God's love to the human race (John 3:16):

> For God so loved the world
>> that he gave his only Son. . . .

Jesus assured His followers in His teaching as well as in giving His life that (John 15:9):

> Just as
>> the Father has loved me
>> I have also loved you.

Furthermore, Jesus confidently stated that (John 14:21):

> He who loves me shall be loved of my father.

Obedience issued out of this love relationship between God and Jesus. Throughout His life this emerged repeatedly as Jesus asserted that (John 4:34) "My food is to do the will of him who sent me. . . ." In the garden of Gethsemane he prayed, facing suffering and death (Matt. 26:39), ". . . not as I will but as you will."

Jesus expects this kind of relationship with those who would be His disciples and claim to love Him. Succinctly He states the principle of obedience (John 15:10):

> If you love me you will obey my commands.

Having exemplified this principle of love and obedience in His own pattern of life, Jesus instructs His followers as to how they can maintain this love relationship (John 15:10):

> If you obey my commands you will remain in my love
>> just as
> I have obeyed my Father's command and remain in his love.

Furthermore, Jesus draws a very distinct line of demarcation between those who love Him and those who don't by asserting that (John 14:23–24):

> Whoever loves me will obey my message
> Whoever does not love me does not obey my word.

Throughout His ministry, Jesus encountered many who wanted to follow Him. Repeatedly He confronted them with a wholehearted commitment in which relatives, material wealth, or any other interest in life must be secondary to their devotion to Him.

The demands in the gospel of Christ were basically the same as those in the gospel of Moses. Both began with a relationship of wholehearted commitment and exclusive devotion which was the basis for obedience. Commandments in the former issue out of the Jesus-man relationship even as commandments in the latter issue out of the God-Israel bond of love. As the Israelites were commanded to love their neighbors because they had been loved and chosen by God, so Jesus commanded His followers that they should love one another because He had chosen them (John 15:16–17).

The command to love one another is addressed to those who have experienced and responded to the love of Jesus and have become His followers. Out of this divine-human relationship comes the capacity to love and on the basis of this, Jesus gives the commandment to His disciples (John 15:9–12):

> This is the law I give you
> You are to love one another as I have loved you.

Jesus significantly concludes His prayer for His followers by appealing to God "that the love you have for me may be theirs (John 17:26).

Love for one another will be the mark of discipleship. Through their display of God-given love for one another all men shall know that they are followers of Jesus Christ.

Paul, an outstanding follower of Jesus Christ, recognized that God's love for man was demonstrated in the death of Christ who as a righteous man died for the ungodly. Speaking about divine love, Paul asserts that "God has poured out his love into our hearts by the Holy Spirit . . ." (Rom. 5:1–11). Writing to the Galatians (2:20) Paul confesses that his faith is "in the Son of God, who loved me and gave himself for me." To the Christians in Corinth (I Cor. 15) Paul points out that they have become Christians through the death and resurrection of Jesus Christ.

As for himself, Paul declares that the love of Christ controls him. Christ's love is the spring of life and the least he can do is to live for Christ (II Cor. 5:14–15). All that matters in life is that faith may find its expression in love (Gal. 5:6).

Paul delineates the concept that love for neighbor is basic in the mutual relationship of those who follow Jesus Christ. Love is the most important of all gifts (I Cor. 13). Heading the list of fruits of the Spirit produced in the life of the God-fearing person is love (Gal. 5:22). In his profound letter to the Romans, Paul expounds concerning man's relationship with God (chaps. 1–11) and man's relationship with his fellow men (chaps. 12–16). Concerning the latter, he admonishes them that they should leave no debt unpaid except the standing debt of mutual love (Rom. 13:8).

In response to the legalism prevailing in Judaism at that time, Paul asserted that love for neighbor is the fulfillment of the law (Rom. 13:10). Writing to the Galatians, Paul advises them that they should serve one another in love (5:12). Against the background of the Old Testament revelation, Paul declares that the entire law is summed up in the commandment, "Love your neighbor as yourself" (5:14). In the context of man's horizontal obligations, this sums up the requirements of the law. In a practical genuine concern for each other they were also fulfilling the law of Christ (Gal. 6:2)—the commandment to love one another as Christ had loved them (John 15:12). To the Corinthians, Paul expressed his concern that they should "make love their great quest" (I Cor. 14:1).

CONCLUSION

Love God with all your heart—the appeal to man is in the gospel of Moses as it is in the gospel of Jesus Christ. Man is endowed with the capacity to respond to God's love for him, the realization of which provides the opportunity for faith and obedience necessary to a vital relationship with God. Says John (I John 4:19):

> We have the power of loving
>   because
> he first had love for us.

The appeal of Moses to his generation was to choose life by loving and obeying God (Deut. 30:19–20). The prophets as represented by Isaiah (55:7) plead with the people who had forsaken God to return to Him who will have mercy on them and abundantly pardon.

The gospel of Jesus Christ is an appeal to respond to God's grace and choose eternal life by recognizing Jesus as the essence of God's love for man. Paul boldly proclaimed that this gospel is the power to save all who believe (Rom. 1:16).

Obedience is the natural sequence in the life of the man who loves God. The commandment to obey—whether given by Moses or by Jesus Christ—is crucial to maintaining this love relationship between man and God. The evidence of this love and obedience toward God is an expression of love toward fellow men. This is the visible and genuine mark of a God-fearing individual according to the gospel of Moses as well as the gospel of Jesus Christ.

God offers His love and mercy to man today as He has since the creation of Adam. The promise in Isaiah (66:1–7) is still applicable. God looks with favor on the one who reveres Him and His Word. Everlasting mercy is promised exclusively to those who love God (Ps. 103:17).

74 75 76 77 10 9 8 7 6 5 4 3 2 1